Three Screenplays

Three Screenplays

Kill List

by Ben Wheatley and Amy Jump

A Field in England

by Amy Jump

&

In the Earth

by Ben Wheatley

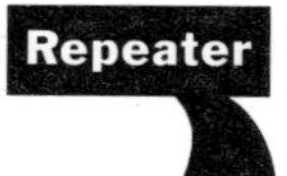

Published by Repeater Books

An imprint of Watkins Media Ltd

Unit 11 Shepperton House

89-93 Shepperton Road

London

N1 3DF

United Kingdom

www.repeaterbooks.com

A Repeater Books paperback original 2026

1

Distributed in the United States by Random House, Inc., New York.

ISBN: 9781917516297

Ebook ISBN: 9781917516303

The manufacturer's authorised representative in the EU for product safety is: eucomply OÜ - Pärnu mnt 139b-14, 11317 Tallinn, Estonia, hello@eucompliancepartner.com, www.eucompliancepartner.com

Printed and bound by CPI Group (UK) Ltd, Croydon, CR0 4YY

Contents

Preface

Dear reader,

Thank you for picking up this compilation of scripts. I hope you enjoy them. They give an interesting insight into the three films. There are missing scenes and different endings and all manner of deviations.

Each of these scripts was written in a different way as well. Amy Jump and I wrote *Kill List*. Amy wrote *A Field in England* and I wrote In the earth. In between these movies we co-wrote *Free Fire,* Amy wrote *High Rise* on her own and I wrote *Happy New Year, Colin Burstead*. So over the years we have changed it up a lot. I think each script has had a different approach. Some were written over an extended period, some written in a frantic month. Sometimes with notes from a studio and financier, some times in a vacuum.

No two experiences are the same.

Kill List

The idea that would become *Kill List* started during the making of the BBC 3 show *The Wrong Door* (2008). *The Wrong Door* was a sketch show that had a vast cast. Usually it's a tight comedy troupe that wear different costumes, *Wrong Door* basically cast different people in every role. I met a lot of actors on that, including the cast of what would become *Kill List*: Neil Maskell, Myanna Buring and Michael Smiley. (Along with Gareth Tunley, the others came from Graham Duff's IDEAL and Jon Link and Mick Bunnage's *Modern Toss.*) I remember wondering what would happen if you teamed Michael, Neil and Myanna together. How would that work? It rolled around my head for a few years. What kind of a movie would that look like?

Myanna had been in Neil Marshall's *The Descent*, and Neil had been in Nick Love's *The Football Factory* and Julian Gilbey's *Rise of the Footsoldier*. To put them together in a movie seemed like the marriage of Horror and Crime genres.

Ideas for films often start as day dreams like this. What if? What if a film was a gunfight? What if a crime family were hiding in plain sight?

Producer Andy Starke had suggested a horror film would be a good thing to make after my first feature film, *Down Terrace* (2009), as there would be a clear route through to an audience. Andy has a film distribution company and knew of a lot of the fantasy and horror film festivals. One of the hardest things for fledgling filmmakers is what to do with your film once you have made it. How do you get it seen?

Andy had a plan. With *Down Terrace* we had a brush with the genre festivals like Fantastic Fest in Austen. With a horror film we could enter it into Spain's Sitges, Toronto's Midnight Madness and Montreal's Fantasia and the Méliès network of fantasy and horror festivals.

So with the basic idea of a crime film that turns into a horror film, I sat down at the kitchen table in the Christmas of 2009, and I set about writing down what scared me; I wrote down nightmares I had as a child. Thinking that if it scared me on a primal level, it would scare an audience.

Amy came into the process after the first draft and added a lot of the more creepy elements to the script, including the victims thanking Jay. We took a lot of the more expositional parts out and brought it down to it's fighting weight.

The film has some improvisation in it, but that was mainly in the form of paraphrasing. So the actors put the lines back into their own words or riffed on the scene.

A Field in England

Amy Jump wrote this script after we completed *Sightseers*. The plan was to make a bigger film, but that fell through. So we decided to make something with a more modest budget.

Amy constructed it so that it could be shot in one location with one set of costumes. She wrote it during the summer of 2012.

This is not a script that was written in close consultation. There were no notes, no development process.

I read it and we made it. I had a similar experience on *High Rise*. I didn't want to mess with her writing. It was too well crafted. My input into this script was: Lets make something during the English Civil War and can it be in the woods, as we had found a great location. (We never did shoot there.)

There is only one line of improvisation in it: "Let's not be cunts," which Ryan Pope threw in. We found that the script was too dense and well written to deviate from. That and the fact that you could never be sure that a word the actors might use was actually in use at that point in time. So on the first day it was clear it was going to be the script and nothing but. This was the first film I shot in which that was the case.

Amy visited the set, but she wasn't around for the whole shoot. Later we edited the movie together. I think the writer-editor hyphenate is a strong one. Joining the prose of the script to the image of the film through one person is a powerful combination.

A Field in England remains my favourite film that I have made. There's something about reading a script and knowing that you are just going to make it. That it is pretty much fully formed. It was shot in chronological order, which was a great treat. So the memory of it is almost a "real" memory. I felt like I was there.

In the Earth

In the Earth was one of three scripts that I wrote during lockdown. It was an obvious reaction to Covid and the weirdness of living in an actual disaster movie. But it was also a reaction to *A Field in England* and to folk horror in general. *Field* had stuck with me, and I felt like I needed to have a conversation with it. In a way, *Free Fire* is also another dig about in the field (a gang of characters in a circle of death). There are rhythms that repeat there as well.

In the Earth was a more direct look at field and at ideas around magic. I felt at the time that narrative itself had been weaponised. You could see day by day how things were being warped out of shape. Reality had been broken and it was something within humans themselves that was the problem. That we join together points of information that don't necessarily have anything to do with each other and call it a story, or worse… a truth. *In the Earth* looks at the "reality" of folk horror, where it might start and end.

I also wanted to make something that put light and sound at the front of the experience. Music and sound design, bright lights and strobes are hard wired into the story. The soundtrack is the story as much as the lighting is. Being a writer-director-editor allows you to do this. It would be pretty hard to bring those elements together if you didn't have complete control of the movie.

It's interesting looking at these old scripts with their battle scars, lost scenes and truncations. Reading the scripts for *Kill List* and *In the Earth*, they have clearly been through a pass of improvisation, and scenes have been compressed or cut in the process. This happens for a number of reasons. Sometimes exposition is written into the script and we know it will likely come out in the edit. Sometimes the film demands it for pace. The script can be manipulated in the edit to make the film a smoother journey.

But then you get a script like *A Field in England* that comes through relatively unchanged.

Thanks for reading,

Ben Wheatley
East Sussex

Introduction

There is a thrill inherent in watching someone in a completely different field to your own succeed at a thing that you have been trying to do with less success. This is partly to do with passing a sanity test; you are no longer alone with your idea, and holding it might not be proof of madness after all. Yet there is a deeper satisfaction, wherein lies the hope that you have learned more about what it is you are attempting by observing a fellow traveller's trajectory to the same destination. Watching *Kill List* for the first time had this sort of effect on me, chiming loudly with the novel I had then completed, and more broadly with my surprise that the list we were building at Zer0 Books appeared to be nearly as concerned with the occult as it was with politics, joining horror's long march from the niche it was historically trapped in, to become a resource and reference that could shed light on areas of knowledge it had been traditionally excluded from.

As with the work of any original, it is never clear at the beginning of a Wheatley/Jump collaboration — and even less so reading these scripts divorced from their filmic context — exactly what it is you have signed up for, an impression that hardens as you are drawn further into their uncompromisingly singular universe. From the outset, assumptions and niches blend and overlap, metastasising and eventually falling into general uselessness as explanatory tools, as no category is quite adequate to the bonfire of genres that each of these scripts occasion. Certainly, at its most reductive, *Kill List* is gripping because of its graphic depictions of physical injury, torture and inexplicable evil, the sheer visceral impact of which necessarily obscures its subtlety and nuance. The inherent horror of the story is not loudly broadcast at the outset; there is no trigger warning that you are entering a "scary" genus and ought to prepare for the grotesque and improbable. Rather, the horror emerges, or seems to, the hints appearing indirect even when they form part of a pattern. Unspoken undertones whisper to previous traumas, and humdrum settings unnerve in their banality. Soon there is noisy understatement, quiet rage and the omnipresence of the moon, an object or worship for a cult and part of a natural countdown to the inevitable denouement, or simply an indifferent witness to another pointless human drama? Wheatley's visual language is as rich as the written scripts, and robbed of their soundtrack the words can read like lyrics without music, telling only half the story, though crucially, I am able to see the films they belong to as I read them, as well as hear the eerie soundtracks hover over the printed word. Similarly, Wheatley's deployment of music is less decorative and more part of the essential atmosphere of his imagined worlds, isolated sound effects existing as part of their embodied reality rather than glorified jump scares employed in a war of attrition with the viewers nerves.

In spite of their wayward exploration of dimensions, all three scripts are grittily plausible. Wheatley's approach is that of a naturalist dealing with the unimaginable in as realistic a way as possible (the "additional dialogue by the cast" helping render the uncanny conversational). This technique is manifest on screen in the person of Neil Maskell, a method actor of ultra-normality, so off the cuff and unaffected that when he does blow, it is a very believable hell that rips forth. As with many of Wheatley's characters/actors, Maskell is both an innocent and a protagonist who has everyone else and only himself to blame. His facial expression following some of the plainest savagery I have seen on screen, as he is crowned for slaying his wife and son by the death cult, is akin to a confused and disappointed infant. He doesn't understand, and neither are we (fully) meant to — although my mishearing him described as one part of a pair of "cocks" (when in fact the client is calling them "cogs") is telling, since his fate is as insultingly personal as it is the product of brute function.

A Field in England ("What do you see friend — nothing, only shadows"), written entirely by Amy Jump, is a lost history told from the point of view of those who seek a "better quality of suffering," the characters the shadows cast by the names and dates that constitute the formal subjects of history. Rather like a dark psychedelic nursery rhyme, these English Civil War deserters' search for an inn is no more illogical than the war they are absenting themselves from, the action hardly moving beyond a handful of copses, before finally forming a circular psychic firing squad reminiscent of the final scene in *The Good The Bad and The Ugly*. The object of their search has been neither a pint nor actual gold, but rather the secrets of alchemy and infinite if oblique levels of understanding. The dialogue, spewed with hatefullest disrelish, is the English of Shakespeare, Milton and *Blackadder 2*. Unsurprisingly, it is the funniest and most artfully executed of the three scripts, its psychedelic underpinnings (hallucinogenic mushrooms being a character in the story) the bridge that connects it to *In the Earth*, the film it feels Wheatley was always building up to make.

Having written a novel about a supernatural plant-monster — and also able to verify the truth of *In the Earth*'s speculations about organic matter seeking to communicate with us through my own mycelial forest walks — the script and film are another instance of watching one's own obsessions through someone else's eyes. Dissonance is integral to the story and its telling, the music of organic life rigged to trees that will literally blow the protagonists minds in a sound and light show controlled by nature herself. From the opening shot, in which we are invited to observe the woods through a circle in a stone pillar, the cameras point-of-view is never necessarily a human one. Instead, it is some other force that is doing the looking, which if anything makes the dialogue even more important, the actors invariably a step behind every inhuman development. Gradually we start to see the forest as it does us, "to give the feeling a face," and discover that the mystical and scientific are simply two sides of the same coin. Wheatley's cosmology is fusion, and the supernatural is also the natural. We don't take the drugs, they take us, their spores moving through the early morning mist to become the very atmosphere itself, where to breathe is to be enlightened.

The film's relatively benign conclusion (for Wheatley) suggests a way out of the darkness and the woods themselves, hinting perhaps at a lighter if not more playful sensibility that would be apparent in his shift towards more mainstream films with unequivocally happier endings. But for those not looking for a path out of the forest, these scripts collect the core concerns and conflicts of one of twenty-first-century Britain's most accomplished auteurs, giving this country back a pagan-punk-psychedelia vision of itself; one where we are watched by strange gods, todays cul-de-sacs are tomorrow's long barrows, and hospital is never a preferable alternative to the folk-ready of involuntary amputation with an axe.

Tariq Goddard
Wiltshire

KILL LIST

INT. JAY'S HOUSE. BEDROOM - EARLY EVENING.

SHEL
(SCREAMING.)
It's all gone.

JAY
How is that possible? There was 40 grand in there.

SHEL
Eight months ago there was 40 grand.

JAY
Eight months! How many fucking scatter cushions do you need.

SHEL
(SCREAMING.)
Don't talk to me like I'm a cunt!

JAY and SHEL look towards the open bedroom door.

(CALLING IN A MOTHERLY VOICE.)
Are you alright, baby?

SAM
(OFF.)
Yeah.

JAY
It doesn't make any sense.

SHEL
Hello!
(FLICKING THE SIDE OF HIS HEAD WITH HER FINGERS.)
You haven't done a days work in 8 months. You've been hiding in that fucking garage.

JAY

Well you'll have to dig into the holiday money to get the jaccuzzi fixed. I can't have that out of action. I need it for my bad back.

SHEL

(SCREAMING.)

Wake up.
There's no holiday money and there's no bad back! It's all in your fucking head.

EXT. JAY'S HOUSE. GARDEN. DAY.

JAY walks around his broken Jacuzzi, one hand on his back another grasping a screwdriver. He creakily reaches down to press the button, with no avail. Nothing happens.

JAY

Fuck.

He looks at the garage and then back at the kitchen window where SHEL stands shaking her head.

INT. JAY'S HOUSE. BATHROOM - EARLY EVENING.

JAY is shaving with a disposable razor. He's listening to the news on a small radio.

SHEL

(SHOUTING OFF.)

Jay!

INT. JAY'S HOUSE. KITCHEN- EARLY EVENING.

SHEL stands in the middle of the kitchen in her in bathrobe with wet hair, surrounded but bags of shopping. Mostly booze and crisps.

INT. JAY'S HOUSE. BATHROOM- EARLY EVENING.

JAY is trying to get ready for the evening. SAM in under his feet in the bathroom, but JAY doesn't mind.

SAM
Why don't girls grow beards?

JAY
Some do.

RADIO
It is the case that in the coming months we will all feel the full brunt of the economic downturn.

SAM
Witches?

SHEL
(OFF.)
Jay!

JAY cuts himself with the razor.

JAY
Fuck.

JAY dabs at his face with the last piece of loo roll to stem the bleeding. He gets blood on the collar of his shirt.

JAY
Yeah, like grandma.

RADIO MP
We may have to make great personal sacrifices to turn this countries fortunes around.

JAY
(TO HIMSELF.)
I bet he won't be sacrificing anything.

INT. JAY'S HOUSE KITCHEN. EARLY EVENING.

SHEL holds the supermarket receipt in JAY's face.

SHEL
Twenty-four tins of tuna?

JAY
There was a deal on. You should have given me a list.

SHEL
I did! You left it on the fridge. Ten bottles of wine?

JAY
You invited them. What the fuck are we going to drink, herbal tea!

SHEL
One hundred and ninety-seven quid. Loo roll?

JAY
(LITTLE BIT PENSIVE.)
Fuck.
(TAKING THE PISS.)
Better not do chilli for dindins then.

SHEL scowls.

JAY
You're in serious danger of turning into a miserable old bitch.
(SHOUTING.)
Sam?

SAM sleepily enters the kitchen in his pajamas.

JAY
Look what I got.

JAY pulls a massive pump-action water pistol out of one of the shopping bags. SAM is ecstatic. SHEL's face is thunderous.

SHEL
Daddy's doing bedtime stories.

JAY looks gutted.

INT. JAY'S HOUSE. KITCHEN - DAY.

SHEL is now dressed, hair dried, gulping back red wine, teary eyed. She's on the phone to her mother venting in Swedish about JAY's inadequacies, oblivious the fact that the dinner is burning behind her on the hob.

INT. JAY'S HOUSE. CHILD'S BEDROOM - EVENING.

SAM's bedroom is jam packed with toys. JAY is crouched uncomfortably on a child-sized plastic chair.

JAY
There was once these two brave and honourable soldiers who were in charge of guarding a man in a car.

SAM
I want a story about King Arthur.

JAY
My story is better.

SAM
No it's not.

JAY
Are you listening, because you can go straight to sleep without?

SAM
What kind of car?

JAY
A bullet-proof one. They were driving around this city, see.

SAM
What city?

JAY
Bagdadistan.

SAM
Which soldier was bravest?

JAY
The good looking one. Listen. So, there were these insurgents and they made a bomb and it blew up the Humvee in front of the column. The soldiers jumped out of their vehicle and started laying down suppressing fire with M14s.

SAM
It's not really though is it.

JAY
Not anymore.

SAM
You shouldn't shout at mummy.

JAY
She started it.

SAM
You're a bit lazy though.

JAY
Who says!

SAM
Mummy.

JAY
Does she now.

SAM
And me.

JAY looks gutted.

JAY
Night, mate.

SAM
Do it, Daddy.

JAY
One two three… Abracadabra.

He clicks his fingers and switches off the light.

SAM
Magic.

Black.

INT. JAY'S HOUSE. HALLWAY - EVENING

The doorbell rings. JAY answers. GAL stands with his back to JAY for a moment before turning to present a broad smile.

JAY
Hello, trouble.

GAL
Matey.

The two men shake hands. We see this in detail. They are wearing rings. They have tattoos on their wrists of dice.

GAL
Long time no see… FIONA, where the fuck are you?

FIONA comes round the corner. She is a little nervous. JAY looks at her. SHEL appears at the door. Big smiles.

FIONA
Hi.

SHEL appears at the front door.

GAL
Sweetheart.

SHEL
(TO FIONA.)
Hi.

FIONA
Fiona.

JAY
(TO FIONA.)
Have we met?

FIONA
I don't know.

GAL
No, you haven't.

SHEL
(COLDLY.)
Let them in, Jay, for Godsake. You're like a brick wall.

FIONA and SHEL go through.

GAL
Brick shit house more like.
(NODDING TO SHEL.)
Everything alright?

JAY
(GRITTED TEETH.)
Couldn't be better.

GAL nods over to FIONA. 'Not bad, eh?' he grins. JAY smiles.

EXT. JAY'S HOUSE. GARDEN - EVENING.

JAY and GAL are poking at a fire pit.

JAY
I can't.

GAL
It's good money.

JAY
Try one of these.

JAY offers GAL a red chili stuffed with feta cheese.

JAY
Blow your fucking head off.

GAL
Nah, I can't eat red food.

JAY
What?

GAL
Just something I'm trying out.

JAY
Have you mentioned it to Shel?

GAL
What, the diet?

JAY
No, the job.

GAL
Maybe in passing.

JAY
No wonder she's been on my fucking back.
Don't do that.

GAL
I wish someone would clarify the chain of command.

SHEL sticks her head out of the back door.

SHEL
Jay!

JAY
Coming.

JAY gets up.

GAL
Scrap that. Clarification received.

JAY
Fuck off.

INT. JAY'S HOUSE. SITTING ROOM - DAY.

FIONA looks at pictures on the wall. GAL and JAY in uniforms in various foreign countries.

FIONA
Argh, sweet.

JAY
Yeah.

FIONA
Must be tough at the moment.

SHEL
We've maintained a loyal client base.

FIONA
You help do you, Shel?

SHEL
Admin. Tax. Invoices. Stuff they can't be bothered with.

FIONA looks at the wall and sees SHEL in uniform as well.

FIONA
Is that you?

SHEL
Swedish National service.

FIONA
I didn't know they made girls do that!

SHEL
I wanted to. I didn't have to. Why should the boys get to have all the fun?

FIONA
Here they both are…

FIONA studies a photo of GAL and JAY in Bagdadistan: Happier times.

FIONA
What uniform is that?

GAL
Security assignment.

FIONA
Sounds dangerous.

GAL
I tell you what, I can't be responsible for the security of your knickers this evening.

FIONA
(LOOKING AT JAY.)
Who says I'm wearing any?

GAL
Urgh! Commando! You filthy bitch!

INT. JAY'S HOUSE. DINING ROOM - EVENING.

FIONA
Human resources.

GAL
Hatchet man. Sorry. Hatchet person.

JAY
You sack them.

FIONA
It's not personal.

JAY
Tell that to their families.

SHEL
(TO JAY.)
When was the last time you cared about the welfare of a family? Oh I know, 8 months ago.

GAL gives JAY a surreptitious glance. JAY grinds his dinner and his teeth.

FIONA
There's a bigger picture in the world of business.

GAL
Your picture doesn't stretch past that front door does it, Jay?

SHEL
(TO JAY.)
You mean the jacuzzi.

(TO FIONA.)
I think the 80s recession was much more glamorous.

FIONA
It's worse this time. A lot of dirty work will have to be done. Cut the wheat from the chaff.

GAL
Sorry, did you say chavs?

INT. JAY'S HOUSE. DINING ROOM - EVENING.

JAY
I'll tell you one lot who had no time fcr extraneous. The Nazi's.

GAL
Here we go.

JAY
I'd' have loved to have had a go at them. It's not easy for a man to know where he stands these days.

SHEL
(TO FIONA.)
To tell the truth, he doesn't do a lot of standing these days. He's worn a hole in the sofa.

JAY points his fork at SHEL threateningly.

GAL
You should have had a crack at 'the mick'. A little tour in Belfast.

FIONA
I never understood all that Irish stuff, it's the same religion isn't it?

GAL
No. Not really, love.

JAY
What the fuck do I get? Iraq!

SHEL
Jesus, fucking Iraq, Iraq is over. What about now? What's going on now, Jay? What about next week when I have to pay for a new school uniform for Sammy?

JAY suddenly pushes his chair back, tips his dinner plate upside down.

JAY
I've finished.

JAY collects each corner of the tablecloth, bundling all their dinners up into a ball, and takes it all into the kitchen, leaving everyone with their mouths open looking at an empty table.

INT. JAY'S HOUSE. CHILD'S BEDROOM - EVENING.

GAL sits on the end of SAM's bed studying one of SAM's swords. The sound of JAY and SHEL screaming at each other emanates up from downstairs.

SAM
Why's mummy and daddy shouting?

GAL
Don't take any notice. They're just over excited.

SAM
Why?

GAL
They drank too much. Don't ever drink, you hear me?

SAM
Not even water?

GAL
Especially not that shit. 'Scuse my French. The government puts stuff in it that shrinks your balls. Just fizzy pop. Promise?

SAM
Promise.

GAL
It's the only thing that's safe.

They sit for a moment listening to the screaming.

GAL (CONT'D)
You've got a lot of kit.

Looking at SAM's sword and shield collection intently.

SAM
Swords are best.

GAL
Guns are better. Didn't your Dad tell you that?

SAM
Swords are.

GAL
Let's see.

GAL forms his hand into a gun and aims as SAM reaches for a toy sword, slashing GAL across the chest. GAL acts mortally injured.

GAL
Fuck me!

SAM
Uncle Gal!

GAL
Shit. Sorry! I have been justly punished.

GAL collapses to the floor.

SAM
Good.

GAL
Tell your mother I loved her.

SAM
What about Dad?

GAL
Tell him whatever you like.

INT. JAY'S HOUSE. KITCHEN - EVENING.

SHEL and FIONA stand awkwardly together in the kitchen, looking at the dinner stuff JAY has dumped along with the tablecloth in the sink. SHEL has obviously been crying. FIONA holds a large glass of white wine up in front of her uncomfortably.

SHEL
Sorry.

FIONA
No. Don't be silly.

There is an uncomfortable moment. This is all too personal for FIONA.

FIONA
How old's your boy?

SHEL
Seven. You?

FIONA
No. I never wanted them.

SHEL
You'll change your mind.

FIONA
No. Don't think so.

There's a sadness about FIONA here.

Love kids though…

SHEL begins digging around in the dismantled dinner. She finds a fork and eats a mouth full of something.

SHEL
He was the one, you know?

FIONA
You mean, the love of your life?

SHEL
No. The one who started the argument. He said I was a miserable old bitch.

FIONA looks away embarrassed. She can't disagree with JAY's assessment. SHEL looks miserably at the plates.

SHEL
These plate cost thirty pound each.

FIONA
They look it.

SHEL
Gal's lovely. Keep hold of him.

INT. JAY HOUSE. GARAGE.

JAY stands alone banging his head against a wall. GAL quietly opens the door.

GAL
Knock. Knock.

GAL and JAY squeeze in amongst exercise machines and other consumer durables. It's a graveyard for impulse purchases. There is a long moment of tense silence. GAL stands waiting for JAY to say what he wants to hear. JAY doesn't want to say it even though he knows he must.

JAY
Where?

GAL
Local. UK.

JAY
How many on the list?

GAL
Three. Not strenuous.

JAY pulls out a machine gun wrapped in wax paper. GAL holds it up to his shoulder.

GAL
How much?

JAY
Don't ask. Shel got it.

GAL
What do you think of Fiona?

JAY
This is the one you met at your sister's?

GAL
No, god no. Met her at Boxercise.

JAY's mood lightens here momentarily. He can't help but be bouyed by GAL's light spirit.

JAY
What?

GAL
Lot of fit women. It's quite empowering… and it relieves sexual tension.

JAY
Fucksake.

GAL throws a few playful punches at JAY's stomach.

GAL
Don't knock it till you've tried it.

JAY
She likes it rough then?

GAL
Wouldn't you like to fucking know.

JAY
I'm too old for that shit, and so are you.

GAL
Speak for your fucking self, grandad.

The atmosphere drops again into another moment of loaded silence. JAY looks away from GAL. Embarrassed to admit the proceeding statement.

JAY
Kiev took it out of me.

GAL
Eight months. It's long enough, right?

JAY
Fuck.

GAL
Get the old team back together. The two musketeers!

They hug.

GAL
Get out. Stretch our legs.

JAY
Yeah.

INT. JAY'S HOUSE. KITCHEN.

GAL and JAY enter the kitchen. GAL winks at SHEL surreptitiously. There is a long moment of tense anticipation.

GAL
(TO SHEL.)
Come on, Mummy, give Daddy a hug.

INT. JAY'S HOUSE. SITTING ROOM.

Everyone is rolling around drunk and laughing hysterically.

INT. JAY'S HOUSE. SITTING ROOM.

Eric Clapton is playing on the sound system. Everyone is slow-dancing.

EXT. JAY'S HOUSE. - NIGHT.

SHEL and JAY stand over the burning fire pit as the flames dance. GAL chases FIONA around the garden. SHEL looks up at SAM's bedroom window.

SHEL
Do you think he heard?

JAY
Course.

SHEL
Maybe I should check he's alright.

JAY puts his arms around his wife. The first moment of tenderness in a long day.

JAY
Sorry.

SHEL
Me too. I just don't want to live on tinned tuna for the rest of my life.

INT. JAY'S HOUSE. BATHROOM - EVENING.

FIONA is on her hands and knees, carving a symbol into the side of the wash cabinet with one of SHEL's best steak knives. Before she leaves the room, FIONA carefully folds one of JAY's blood-splattered toilet roll clods, discarded after that morning's shaving cut. She stuffs it in the cup of her bra with satisfaction.

INT. JAY'S HOUSE. HALLWAY - NIGHT.

FIONA totters down the stairs. GAL is climbing into his cowboy hat. FIONA gives SHEL a hug and kisses JAY on the lips. It is obvious that JAY is sober. He watches the others stagger down the path with mild contempt.

GAL
Cheers, mate.

JAY
You're not driving.

GAL
When I find my keys.

Looking through the multiple pockets in his flak jacket.

JAY
Shel? Call a cab.

SHEL stumbles off to the phone.

GAL
The fuck you will.

JAY
I'll drop the car in the morning.

GAL
The fuck you will.

JAY
Why do you have such a problem following orders?
(JAY COMES UP CLOSE TO GAL'S EAR.)
Don't go behind my back to her again.

EXT. JAY'S HOUSE. PAVEMENT- NIGHT.

JAY and GAL are rolling around punching the shit out of each other as the cab pulls up. SHEL opens the cab door and FIONA tumbles in. JAY bundles GAL in behind and slams the door. GAL comes up confused.

GAL
You tore my fucking jeans.

The cab speeds off. SHEL and JAY stand for a moment in the sudden silence of the night.

JAY
Thank fuck that's over.

INT. JAY'S HOUSE. BEDROOM - NIGHT.

JAY sits bolt upright. SHEL is sleeping deeply next to him. He gets out of bed and draws the curtain. The moon is bright.

INT. JAY"S HOUSE. KITCHEN - NIGHT.

JAY pulls the ice tray from the freezer and chucks a fistfull of cubes into a large whiskey. He stops for a moment distracted by the family's pet cat, Lulu, crossing the garden. She looks at him. He waves slowly.

INT. JAY'S HOUSE. BEDROOM - MORNING.

JAY awakes to find SAM jumping up and down on top of him.

JAY
What! No!

INT. JAY'S HOUSE. KITCHEN - MORNING.

SHEL is on her mobile phone, pacing up and down. There is no evidence of last night's party.

JAY OFF/SCREEN
Shel!

SHEL
(TO PHONE.)
That's no problem. They'll be there.

JAY O/S
Shel!

SHEL hangs up her phone.

EXT. JAY'S HOUSE. GARDEN - MORNING.

JAY stands over a small pile of intestines in the middle of the lawn.

JAY
She's done it again.

JAY and SHEL look at Lulu the cat, who sits contentedly observing them.

SHEL
(TO LULU THE CAT)
That's the last time, you hear me, you little shit!

JAY
It's an offering, not an insult.

SHEL
She's taking the piss.

JAY
It's a cat - it can't take the piss.

SHEL
What is it?

JAY stoops down, digs his fingers around in the bloody pulp and licks them.

JAY
Rabbit.

SHEL
Jay!

JAY scoops the guts up and marches off to the kitchen.

SHEL
Put it in the outside bin.

JAY
Fuck am I? I'm going to fry it up with a bit of onion and garlic.

SHEL
Not in my kitchen!

EXT. JAY'S HOUSE. KITCHEN - MORNING.

JAY sits in the middle of the lawn on a deck chair facing the house. SHEL and SAM watch him through the window as he eats his fried kill with uncertain relish.

SAM
What's Daddy doing?

SHEL
Showing off.

EXT. ROADS - DAY.

JAY drives GAL's car down a dual carriageway. The city is muted. Discordant music stirs with foreboding. The landscape is toneless. Nothing seems to move except JAY.

INT. GAL'S CAR - DAY.

JAY listens for a minute to more news about the economic downturn.

RADIO
At first it was presumed that the banking sectors, financial and business services would bear the brunt of the recession, but as new figures released today reveal, it's the blue collar, manual workers that have

been hardest hit by unemployment. It was thought that this recession would see women suffering in the workplace worse than men. But the statistics do not bear this out. The number of men in work has fallen by 3%, the number of women by 0.8%.

His eye is distracted from the road ahead by a hazy rainbow in the sky. He turns the radio off.

EXT. GAL'S HOUSE - DAY.

GAL opens the front door before JAY knocks. Several security cameras are trained on the front door. GAL's house is a fortified 60s council box. The front garden is dominated by a motorbike covered in tarp. GAL wears combat shorts and large comedy slippers. They contrast sharply with his sullen expression.

GAL
Kettle's just boiled.

JAY
Fiona?

GAL
Gone.

JAY
Off deforcing?

GAL
Fuck knows.

JAY
What?

GAL
I may have done something wrong. I woke up with a 'Dear John' gaffer-taped to my cock.

JAY
You're kidding.

GAL
Where does a woman find a typewriter in the middle of the night, I ask you?

JAY
Get your shit together, client's expecting us.

GAL
Take me to the cash cow.

INT. HIT CAR NO 1. HOTEL CAR PARK - DAY.

The car's side windows are obscured by several hanging suit bags. JAY and GAL are dressed for work and ready for action. GAL pulls a sports bag from the back seat. JAY surveys the car's interior, running his hand across leather.

JAY
Nice.

GAL
It's a dog on corners.

GAL opens the bag to reveal two pistols.
JAY frowns.

GAL
Better safe than sorry.

GAL hands JAY a pistol.

JAY
I haven't got a holster.

GAL
Stick it in your trousers.

JAY gives GAL a look of contempt.

INT. HOTEL NO 1. RECEPTION - DAY.

GAL and JAY make their way through faded grandeur.

THE RECEPTIONIST looks up but does not question their presence.

INT. HOTEL NO. 1. BALLROOM - DAY.

GAL and JAY walk into a large ballroom. A man sits nonchalantly drinking tea at a table. They walk over to him. He looks them up and down and then smiles. He gets up and beckons them to follow him.

INT. HOTEL NO 1. CORRIDORS - DAY.

JAY, GAL and THE CLIENT walk down a seemingly endless corridor.

INT. HOTEL NO 1. SUITE - DAY.

The room is cast in shadow. THE CLIENT is silhouetted against chintz and heavily carved wood.

CLIENT
You come with recommendations.

JAY
They're well earned.

CLIENT
It's a good feeling. A necessary feeling.

THE CLIENT points to a pile of currency on the table. He writes a list of names, folds the paper and places it on top of the money.
JAY leans slowly forward. As he reaches for the money and list, THE CLIENT cuts JAY's hand with a small knife. There is a moment when everyone freezes. THE CLIENT wipes JAY's blood on headed paper. (Headed with the name of a bank.) GAL has drawn his pistol.

JAY
It's alright.

GAL
No it's not.

THE CLIENT cuts his own hand with the knife. His blood drips on the paper. He folds it and puts in an envelope. An employee appears and takes the envelope away.

CLIENT
I hear Kiev was stormy.

JAY
I'm in the process of rewriting it.

CLIENT
Good. It's important to learn from one's mistakes.

THE CLIENT gets up and leaves. There's a moment of silence. GAL holsters his gun.

GAL
Fuck.

GAL slumps in THE CLIENT'S chair.

GAL
That was dramatic.

JAY
I'm bleeding on the carpet.

JAY goes into the bathroom to run his hand under the tap while GAL eats complimentary mints and counts the money.

GAL
None of them ever say please or thank you. Have you noticed? That's what irritates me.

JAY wraps his hand in toilet roll.

GAL (CONT'D)
I mean manners don't cost anything, do they?

JAY
How did he know about Kiev?

GAL
He was letting us know that he knew…

JAY
What does that mean?

GAL
Psychology.

GAL points to his head.

INT. JAY'S HOUSE. KITCHEN - DAY.

JAY stands at the kitchen window drinking tea, silently observing SHEL in the garden. She is engrossed in a conversation with a builder who makes notes and suggestions about the conservatory.

INT. JAY'S HOUSE. BATHROOM - DAY.

JAY unwraps the bandage on his hand and examines the knife wound. It's already red and angry. He fumbles around in the medicine cabinet reading labels and finally drowns it in TCP.

SHEL O/S
He said he could start at the end of the month.

JAY
Yeah?

SHEL
I was thinking the whole length on the house. I mean, if you're going to do something, might as well go the whole hog.

JAY
Just make sure it's got plenty of curtains.

SHEL
Jay! It's a conservatory!

JAY
I like curtains. And I like them closed.

INT. JAY'S HOUSE. GARAGE - DAY.

JAY is dressed in his work suit. He hugs SHEL.

INT. JAY'S HOUSE. HALLWAY - DAY.

JAY, SHEL and SAM are at the open front door. GAL is parked at the curb with the engine running.

SAM
I don't want you to go.

JAY
Look at me. I'm a monkey in a suit.

JAY distracts his son with a monkey impersonation.

SHEL
Do a good job.

SHEL kisses JAY.

JAY
Look. I really was just having a rest.

INT. HIT CAR NO. 1 - DAY.

GAL pulls away. JAY watches with emotion as his family disappear into the distance.

GAL
I love this bit.

JAY
We're not going to the fucking seaside.

GAL
Well sorry but I couldn't wait. I ate my sandwich.

GAL holds up an empty packet.

GAL
Managed to save some of yours though.

GAL tosses JAY a half-eaten cheese roll.

INT. HOTEL NO 2. RECEPTION - AFTERNOON.

GAL and JAY check into a business hotel on the outskirts of town. THE RECEPTIONIST is generic and impersonal. A corporate automaton.

RECEPTIONIST
Here on business?

GAL
Crackers.

RECEPTIONIST
Excuse me?

GAL
Novelty key rings. Paper hats. Plastic fingernails. Doggy charms. They're my speciality.

RECEPTIONIST
Sorry?

GAL
You wouldn't be love.

JAY rolls his eyes.

RECEPTIONIST
You don't look like sales.

JAY
Is the Wi-Fi free?

RECEPTIONIST
No.

JAY
Fuck.

INT. HOTEL NO 2. JAY'S ROOM - DAY.

GAL and JAY consult the list. JAY rips open an envelope, takes out a photo and studies it for a moment, before moving to the window and peering out. Nothing but car park and scrubland as far as the eye can see.

GAL
Philip Durrant, 45. 23 Goldwater Road. That's it. Bit thin, isn't it?

JAY picks up this binoculars and focuses on a distant conservatory. He shakes his head with contempt.

JAY
It's enough.

JAY is poking about. He goes into the bathroom.

JAY
Soap's nice.

GAL
Is it still in the wrapper?

JAY
Yeah.

GAL
Good. I fucking hate dirty soap. You want to watch this fella for a bit? See what he gets up to?

JAY
Do it properly, you mean. Not just mow him down in a hail of bullets like some Hackney crackhead.

GAL
Yeah

JAY
Okay

INT. HOTEL NO 1. RESTAURANT - EVENING.

JAY and GAL sit at a small, cramped table. The restaurant is deserted except for a group of approximately 6 people who have been seated nearby. GAL and JAY are trying to eat but can't tune out of their conversation.

GAL
Look at the place…

JAY looks around unimpressed.

GAL
It's a graveyard. And they're right fucking next to us. Why?

WOMAN 1
I just wanted to say 'thank you' to Justin. His teachings have helped me put everything in perspective. I haven't had an anxiety attack in three weeks.

GAL
Don't listen.

JAY
It's like a fucking worm boring through my skull.

JAY looks through the window as he chews meditatively.

MAN 1
Kiera's right to be proud. I've seen a real change in her since she really began to listen.

WOMAN 1
Thanks, Stuart.

MAN 1
I think you'd be the first to agree, Keira, that you're a lot less self-serving.

GAL nearly chokes on his steak.

JAY
You think she's alright?

JAY looks pained. He peers around at THE WOMAN.

GAL
She's lapping it up.

MAN 1
That's why I thought you might intersect with the group, when I saw you having trouble rationalizing your emotional response to Duncan's departure.

GAL
I'd like to see him rationalize your emotional response.

JAY
Don't.

JUSTIN
It makes me really thankful to hear you both speak with such love and respect.

INT. HOTEL NO 2. RESTAURANT - EVENING.

GAL sneaks up behind THE WAITRESS, who is sorting cutlery.

GAL
Love can you put some music on before my friend breaks that man's jaw?

WAITRESS
Sound system's broken.

GAL turns - distracted by the sounds of a guitar's gentle strum.

GAL
Here we go...

GAL looks over at JAY, who shakes his head despairingly.

INT. HOTEL NO 2. RESTAURANT - EVENING.

JUSTIN and his group smile warmly at each other.

INT. HOTEL NO 2. RESTAURANT - EVENING.

JAY
Would it be wrong to kill them?

GAL
I wouldn't like to say.

INT. HOTEL NO 2. RESTAURANT - EVENING.

JUSTIN
Onward, Christian soldiers,
Marching as to war,
With the cross of Jesus
Going on before.
Christ, the Royal Master,
Leads against the foe;
Forward into battle
See His banners go!

INT. HOTEL NO 2. RESTAURANT - EVENING.

JAY and GAL are withering.

GAL
I miss being in a gang.

JAY
The army's not a gang. Besides we're a gang.

GAL
You can't be a gang with just two people.

JAY
It's already one too many for my liking.

GAL
Fuck off!

JAY
Next you'll want matching jumpers.

JAY looks over at JUSTIN and his gang. Their contentedness feels like a personal insult.

GAL
Look at the happy fuckers.

JAY
You could always go and join them.

GAL is quite getting into the music. Perhaps he sings along. Just to irritate JAY. JAY is increasingly tense.

JUSTIN
(SINGING DURING ABOVE DIALOG.)
Onward, Christian soldiers,
Marching as to war,
With the cross of Jesus
Going on before.

At the sign of triumph
Satan's host doth flee;
On then, Christian soldiers,
On to victory!
Hell's foundations quiver
At the shout of praise;
Brothers, lift your voices,
Loud your anthems raise.

JAY reaches his limit of tolerance. He strides over

to JUSTIN and grabs his guitar.

GAL
(TO HIMSELF.)
Here we go.

JAY
You're giving me indigestion.

JUSTIN
I'm sorry.

JAY
Apology accepted.

JUSTIN
Sometimes God's love is hard to swallow.

JAY
Not as hard as a dinner plate.

JUSTIN
God loves you.

JAY is about to break the guitar.

JAY
Tell God from me, if you're the kind cf people he hangs around with, he better stay out of my way.

JAY wants to hit someone but can't justify it. All he's offered is contented smile.
There's a long moment. JAY chucks the guitar back into JUSTIN's lap.
Seething, he leaves the dining room without looking back.
GAL corners THE WAITRESS.

GAL
A round of drinks for my friends.
(TO JUSTIN.)
Put a word in for me with the big man, will you?

GAL points to the sky and runs after JAY. JUSTIN resumes his song. The music continues over the following.

INT. HOTEL NO. 2. CORRIDOOR - NIGHT.

JAY and GAL walk down dimly lit corridors.

Like a mighty army
Moves the church of God;
Brothers, we are treading
Where the saints have trod.
We are not divided,
All one body we,
One in hope and doctrine,
One in charity.

INT. HOTEL NO 2. GAL'S ROOM - NIGHT.

GAL strips and cleans his pistol. He looks blankly ahead.

What the saints established
That I hold for true.
What the saints believed,
That I believe too.
Long as earth endureth,
Men the faith will hold,
Kingdoms, nations, empires,
In destruction rolled.

INT. HOTEL NO 2. JAY'S ROOM - NIGHT.

JAY sets out his toiletries. He is very particular. He folds and unfolds his clothes. He takes out of his bag a pillow case. He takes the hotel pillow case off and replaces it with his own. JAY washes his wound and takes some pills.

Crowns and thrones may perish,
Kingdoms rise and wane,
But the church of Jesus
Constant will remain.

Gates of hell can never
Gainst that church prevail;
We have Christ's own promise,
And that cannot fail.

EXT. HOTEL NO 2. CAR PARK - NIGHT.

The car park is lifeless. Nothing and no one comes or goes. The wind blows leaves and litter. Something watches.

Onward then, ye people,
Join our happy throng,
Blend with ours your voices
In the triumph song.
Glory, laud and honor
Unto Christ the King,
This through countless ages
Men and angels sing.

EXT. COLDWATER RD - DAY.

GAL and JAY are hunkered down in the car observing a man as he enters and exits a substantial property. He's packing the boot of his car. On his last exit he is dressed as a Catholic priest.

JAY
Well that answers the riddle of who contestant number one is.

GAL frowns. It's not what he wanted.

INT. ST. STEVEN'S CHURCH - DAY.

JAY walks through the building with a nonchalant air of confidence. He opens doors and cupboards. Takes notes. No one seems to see him.

EXT. ST. STEVEN'S CHURCH - DAY.

JAY and GAL sit contemplating the church's facade. GAL is uncharacteristically reserved. The cross looms large in his consciousness. JAY's focus is directed at a Cornish pasty.

JAY
You're worried.

GAL
Maybe.

JAY
He's probably shagging kids. It will probably get you a pass on all the other terrible shit you've done.

GAL
It's complicated.

JAY
As a parent, I'd do them all. Even if I wasn't getting paid.

GAL
For the record, I've hardly done any terrible shit.

JAY
You could confess or whatever, before, if you like.

GAL
I'd have to tell him I was about to kill him!

JAY
Fuck - I don't know.

GAL
Fine. We'll kill a priest and go to hell.
(PAUSE.)
I don't know how you eat those things.

INT. ST. STEVEN'S CHURCH - DAY.

The Priest conducts his sermon.

EXT. ST. STEVEN'S CHURCH - DAY.

JAY and GAL break open a door.

INT. ST. STEVEN'S CHURCH - DAY.

The congregation are singing. This is all mute. Atmospheric music plays instead.

INT. ST. STEVEN'S CHURCH - DAY.

JAY and GAL walk down the corridors that JAY scoped previously. He knows where he is going and GAL follows.

EXT. ST. STEVEN'S CHURCH - DAY.

The congregation are leaving. Many shake THE PRIEST's hand respectfully. Once the last person has gone, THE PRIEST lights a cigarette.

INT. ST. STEVEN'S CHURCH - DAY.

JAY and GAL open the church office's door.

INT. ST. STEVEN'S CHURCH - DAY.

THE PRIEST tidies the church.

INT. ST. STEVEN'S CHURCH - EVENING.

JAY and GAL look around the office. GAL looks out of the window and opens it. He looks down and can see their car.

INT. ST. STEVEN'S CHURCH - EVENING.

THE PRIEST is walking along the corridor. He reaches his office door and opens it.

INT. ST. STEVEN'S CHURCH OFFICE - EVENING.

THE PRIEST enters his office nonchalantly, thinking he is alone. JAY and GAL are nowhere to be seen. Only when THE PRIEST sits down does he notice the sheet of plastic covering his desk.
JAY raises his gun to shoot. The phone rings. THE PRIEST answers it.

PRIEST
Yes. Everything is on course. No, no… he isn't. But he will be, any minute.

THE PRIEST hangs up. He turns slowly in his chair to face GAL and JAY, out of shot, without surprise. He smiles warmly.

JAY
Turn around.

PRIEST.
Thank you.

THE PRIEST turns away from them, still smiling.
We hear the 'thwap' of a silencer. A red flower of flesh appears on THE PRIEST's face. He slumps onto the desk. His attache case splits open and photo

graphs fall out. GAL quickly zips the body into a body bag.
GAL and JAY throw the body out of the window. It lands with a heavy thud by the car. JAY grabs the attache case and holds up photographs depicting some kind of murder.

EXT. ST. STEVEN'S CHURCH - EVENING.

JAY and GAL heave the body into the boot of the car.

They jump in and drive away.

INT. HIT CAR NO. 1 - NIGHT.

JAY and GAL drive through the city.

GAL
Killing a priest. My mother will turn in her grave. She was very religious.

JAY
Yeah, I remember, 'Jesus Christ' this, 'fucking hell' that.

GAL
I might throw up.

JAY
Don't. It's done. He's in heaven now. So it's a win-win situation.

GAL
We're in major shit with the big man.

JAY pulls the car over suddenly, pulls on the hand-brake and turns to GAL.

JAY
Gal. We agreed mate. In a fucking sand hole in the desert. God doesn't exist. There's nothing. Just this.

GAL
I know. I know.

JAY
Then how can you be scared of nothing?

GAL
I know.

GAL looks out the window. He's trying to agree with JAY but it's a struggle.

JAY
I'm just doing my job. What are you doing?

GAL
I'm already over it.

JAY
Good.

JAY restarts the engine and the car moves into the flow of traffic.

EXT. WORKSHOP - NIGHT.

JAY and GAL drive into an industrial unit.

INT. WORKSHOP - NIGHT.

JAY and GAL stuff the body into a raging furnace. Their faces glowing in the light of the blaze.

JAY
Why did he smile like that do you think?

GAL
Probably at peace, you know.

JAY
I'm not sure how peaceful being shot in the back of the head is.

GAL
When put like that...

INT. WORKSHOP - NIGHT.

GAL is leafing through the photos from the Priest's briefcase.

JAY
Why did you pick that up?

GAL shrugs. GAL looks at a man hung under a bridge. Another image shows a burnt man. There is foreign text.

GAL
Latin?

JAY
Fuck knows.

GAL
Just interested.

JAY
It's nothing to do with us.

GAL
Looks like he was nosing about in someone else's business.

GAL raises a delicate sheet of paper. The furnaces warm glowing light illuminates the image of a knight.

JAY
Sam would like that.

GAL
Do you think you should give him a dead man's stuff?

JAY
It's our stuff now.

JAY takes the knight and carefully folds and pockets it. The suspect photos he throws into the furnace without a second thought.

JAY
I better call Shel. Give her an update. You know what she's like about schedules.

GAL
She hasn't called…

JAY
Shel?

GAL
Fiona.

JAY
How much apologizing have you done?

GAL
None. I don't know what I did wrong!

JAY
Fuck sake. It doesn't matter! 'Sorry' and 'Thank You'.That's all you've got to keep saying.

JAY shakes his head pityingly.

JAY
Christ! You're worrying about what God thinks. He's not going to cook your fucking dinner for you, is he?

GAL
Sorry. Thank You.

JAY
Let's just focus on the job and we'll order your Thai bride later.

GAL throws the attache case in the fire.

GAL
That's not a bad idea. I bet Thai brides are filthy.

EXT. HOTEL NO. 3 - DAY.

JAY and GAL pull up in front of another sterile business hotel. The drone of the dual carriage way is never escaped. A few suited men huddle over lap-tops in the hotel bar.

INT. HOTEL NO. 3 - RECEPTION.

The reception is dimly lit and silent. THE RECEP-TIONIST is Thai.

RECEPTIONIST
Good afternoon. Can I help?

JAY
Have the rooms got free Wi-Fi?

RECEPTION
No, sir.

JAY
Bollocks.

GAL
Are you married?

INT. HOTEL NO. 3. JAY'S ROOM - LATE AFTERNOON

JAY has unpacked his modest hand luggage. Everything is laid out on the bed. The T.V. is on mute. JAY's at the desk adjusting the laptop camera as it con-nects to Skype.
SHEL answers.

JAY
Can you see me?

SHEL
I was just asleep.

JAY
Sorry.

SHEL
Sam was up in the night.

JAY
He alright?

SHEL
Bad dreams about the cat. What's the room like? I couldn't tell when I booked.

JAY
It's alright.

SHEL
You on schedule.

JAY
One down.

SHEL
Clean?

JAY
Of course. Don't worry, I'm alright.

SHEL
Sam, it's your Dad.

SAM looks right in the camera.

SAM
Hi, Dad.

JAY
Hi, mate.

SAM
When are you coming home?

JAY
Soon.

SAM
Okay. Bring me a present.

SAM runs off.

SHEL
Fiona turned up unannounced. She bought a toy for Sammy.

JAY
Odd. Gal hasn't heard from her.

SHEL
I didn't like her at first, but I don't mind her now. What do you think?

JAY
You could do with a bit of company.

SHEL
That's what I thought.

JAY
Just keep her out of the garage.

SHEL
I'm not an idiot.

JAY
I know but…

SHEL
I've got to go anyway. Sam's on the loo.

JAY
Okay. Love you. Speak later.

JAY closes the laptop and carefully lays down on the bed next to his possessions.

INT. HOTEL NO. 3. JAY'S BATHROOM - DAY.

JAY leans over the sink. His shirt hangs on the bathroom door. The bandage on his cut hand is grimy. He removes it with care to reveal a very tender, irritated wound. Even though he knows he shouldn't, he prods and pokes it until pus seeps out. He looks at the sparse bathroom shelf: A tiny bottle of shampoo, a tiny bottle of bubble bath, a tiny bottle of body lotion. He squeezes some of the body lotion onto the wound and wraps the soiled bandage back round it.

INT. HOTEL NO. 3. GAL'S ROOM - DAY.

GAL is in his pants and socks, spread out on his wrecked bed, watching a documentary about the Second World War. The room is already a scene of devastation with empty food and drink cartons everywhere. A big box of chocolates is balanced on his stomach and a can of beer lies on the pillow next to him. He rubs his temples and takes some pills.

GAL goes into the bathroom and puts a shower cap over the smoke sensor. He lights a cigarette and sits in the toilet for a shit. He peruses the photo of the dead priest. He takes out a small candle. Lights it and burns the photo. He drops the picture in the bath.

He contemplates the candle for a bit before snuffing it out with his hand. He crosses himself.

EXT. HOTEL NO. 3 - NIGHT.

GAL looks out of his window.

INT. HOTEL NO. 3 RESTAURANT - MORNING.

GAL and JAY are having breakfast.

JAY
Not bad.

GAL
Sausage is tasteless. But the bacon is definitely bacon.

JAY
It is.

GAL
Why would you smile when you're about to get strung up on a tree?

JAY
What?

GAL
Those photos, the priest had.

JAY
I know what you mean. It's not right. But it's done. I don't know what everyone's got to be so fucking cheery about. I mean, look at that…

JAY signals to a happy couple chatting and giggling over their continental breakfast.

GAL
Don't start.

EXT. SUBURBAN LANDSCAPE - DAY.

JAY and GAL cruise through an affluent residential area. They are in a different vehicle now. The houses are impressive and they study each property with guarded jealousy.

JAY
I reckon £500k plus.

GAL
I wouldn't live here.

JAY
My arse!
GAL
No, I don't like it, it feels wrong. Too perfect.

JAY
We're being tailed.

GAL
Which?

JAY
Maroon Sierra, two cars back.

GAL
You mean Mondeo. They haven't built a Sierra since the 90s.

JAY
Fuck, Mondeo then.

JAY steers the car into the driveway of an affluent property at random.

EXT. POSH HOUSE. DRIVEWAY - DAY.

JAY and GAL get out and stretch their legs.

GAL
Something bad happened here. The vibe's bad.

JAY
If it hasn't already, it might do soon.

GAL
You can't pave over sorrow. It seeps through the cracks.

JAY
How do you feel about sandstone? Shel wants it instead of decking.

GAL
I'm pro decking.

JAY
She thinks it rots.

EXT. POSH HOUSE - DAY.

Time has shifted slightly. JAY is smoking a cigarette.

GAL
My dream home is an island.

JAY
Northern Ireland?

GAL
No, *an* island. Deserted. Easy to defend.

JAY
How the fuck are you going to meet women on an island.

GAL
Obviously I'd have to be able to commute. And be near bars and a cinema.

JAY
A tropical island just off Kent then?

GAL
It's people that spoil places. I hate them. I feel this fucking rage welling up and I want to kill them.

JAY
You are in the right job then.

GAL
I only feel like myself when I'm out in the woods.

JAY
I know what you mean, mate.

GAL
Any movement?

JAY
Negative.

EXT. URBAN AREA - DAY.

JAY and GAL's car glides through town. The buildings are lackluster. Every other business has closed down.

INT. HIT CAR NO. 2 BY LOCK-UPS - DAY.

The car is parked up the street from a row of lock-ups. GAL is studying a photo of the target.

GAL
This guy looks like nothing.

JAY
They all look like nothing.

GAL
Actually, he looks a bit like my Uncle Terry.

JAY
Was Uncle Terry nice?

GAL
Not really.

JAY
That should make things easier then.

GAL
Here he comes.

THE LIBRARIAN walks over to a lock-up and starts fiddling with keys.

INT. HIT CAR NO. 2 - DAY.

JAY eats a Cornish pasty and ponders.

JAY
Have you spoken to Fiona yet?

GAL
No.

JAY
She's been round to ours, crying on Shel's shoulder.

GAL
Really?

JAY
She's waiting. That's what she said.

GAL
For me?

JAY
Who else?

GAL
Should I leave her dangling a bit longer?

JAY
Just ring. I don't want to find Shel's new best friend has moved into my spare room.

INT. HIT CAR NO. 2 - DAY.

GAL snores. The man comes out of the lock-up and walks off without any idea that he is being observed. JAY nudges GAL awake.

GAL
Go?

JAY
I want to see what's in that lock-up first.

GAL
I thought you were only interested in the names.

INT. LOCKUP - DAY.

JAY and GAL break into the lock-up. Strip lights blink into life. The place is a sea of mouldy old porn mags, piles of books, manuscripts, tapes, DVD's. There is a sense of disorganised logic to it. The only clear space is right in the centre, were an easy chair sags in front of a television and various decks.

JAY
Nice… it's a wank den.

GAL
Wanking never got anyone shot.

They poke around. GAL finds a VHS and DVD duplication bay.

GAL
Porno business?

JAY shakes his head.

GAL turns on the DVD player. An image flickers into life.
We don't see what the DVD relays, but GAL's expression illustrates the horror of it. He quickly turns it off.

GAL
Fuck.

JAY
What?

GAL
Don't.

JAY
Well I'll have to now.

JAY turns on the DVD. He watches for a few moments. He looks horrified. He turns it off. He starts to cry.

INT. THE LIBRARIAN'S HOUSE - LATE AFTERNOON.

GAL and JAY approach the front door with purpose and knock. The man previously seen entering and leaving the lock-up opens the door.

LIBRARIAN
Yes?

JAY and GAL flash fake Police IDs.

JAY
Inspector Dreyfuss and Inspector Harris, can we have a word?

LIBRARIAN
Sorry, concerning?

JAY
There's been a few burglaries around here in the last 24 hours.

LIBRARIAN
Haven't seen anything.

GAL
We'd like to step inside and clarify a few details with you.

LIBRARIAN
There's nothing to clarify, I don't know anything.

JAY
You'd be surprised what you can remember when you're memory is given a jolt.

GAL looks down the street. JAY punches the man in the stomach. He falls back into the house.

LIBRARIAN
Help.

JAY
Not for you, son.
JAY kicks the man unconscious.

INT. LIBRARIAN'S HOUSE - LATE AFTERNOON.

The man is tied to a chair.

LIBRARIAN
There's been a mistake.

GAL
Oh?

LIBRARIAN
Mistaken identity.

GAL
We'll, we've just remembered that we're the burglars.

LIBRARIAN
Really? If you are - take what you want.

GAL
What have you got?

LIBRARIAN
Everything, everything.

GAL
What do you need, Jay? Personally I could do with a bit of reassurance that the world's not full of murdering perverts.

JAY
We saw the lock-up.

The man begins to weep.

JAY
Don't bother.

GAL
I don't know why you are crying, I saw one of your little films. I can't un-see that.

LIBRARIAN
I'm
just the librarian. I'm not responsible for compiling the documentation.

GAL
Who for?

LIBRARIAN
This is not fair.

JAY
I'll show you 'not fair'.

JAY hits the man across the face.

INT. THE LIBRARIAN'S HOUSE. KITCHEN - LATE AFTERNOON.

The man is bloody.
JAY punches him again to get his attention.
GAL winces.

LIBRARIAN
Please

JAY
Don't. It makes me hate you more.

LIBRARIAN
I'll tell you who films it.

GAL
Let's have it.

LIBRARIAN
He's at 15 Greenwold street.

GAL
Where's your money stashed?

INT. LIBRARIAN'S HOUSE. STAIRCASE - LATE AFTERNOON.

GAL runs upstairs.

INT. LIBRARIAN'S HOUSE. KITCHEN - LATE AFTERNOON.

THE LIBRARIAN is covered in blood and burn marks. JAY has been at work for some time, yet, as soon as GAL leaves the room, THE LIBRARIAN's demeanor changes markedly. Petrified fear is replaced by a sober, almost conspiratorial affability.

LIBRARIAN
Does he know?

JAY
(CONFUSED.)
What?

LIBRARIAN
Who you are. He doesn't, does he?

JAY
What the fuck are you talking about?

LIBRARIAN
Before he comes back, I just want to say thank you.

JAY
For what?

LIBRARIAN
I am glad to have met you.

INT. LIBRARIAN'S HOUSE. BEDROOM - LATE AFTERNOON.

GAL has opened a small safe in which he has found money and a portfolio. He grabs it all. We can hear THE LIBRARIAN screaming in the background.

GAL
(SHOUTING.)
Got it.

INT. LIBRARIAN'S HOUSE. KITCHEN - LATE AFTERNOON.

LIBRARIAN
I understand that you have to do what you have to do.

JAY grabs a hammer out of a toolbox in the kitchen. He slams the hammer down on THE LIBRARIAN's leg. THE LIBRARIAN screams. JAY smashes his knees.

JAY
You shut up now.

INT. LIBRARIAN'S HOUSE. BEDROOM - LATE AFTERNOON.

GAL listens to the screaming. He's letting it happen. He knows it's wrong.

INT. LIBRARIAN'S HOUSE. KITCHEN - LATE AFTERNOON.

JAY grabs THE LIBRARIAN's hand and pins it down to the table. He takes the hammer and slams THE LIBRARIAN's fingers backwards. The man screams.

LIBRARIAN
Thank you.

JAY
Shut up.

INT. LIBRARIAN'S HOUSE. BEDROOM - LATE AFTERNOON.

GAL rubs his face. He can hear the hammering and the screaming.

INT. LIBRARIAN'S HOUSE. KITCHEN - LATE AFTERNOON.

JAY stands behind THE LIBRARIAN and smashes the hammer down. The man's head splits open. JAY hammers it into oblivion.

JAY
You crazy fucking bastard.

GAL comes down and sees what JAY has done.

GAL
Fuck.

INT. LIBRARIAN'S HOUSE - LATE AFTERNOON.

GAL and JAY zip the body into a body bag.

GAL
You can clean that shit up.

JAY
Fine.

GAL
I told you about this in Kiev.

INT. HIT CAR NO. 2 - DUSK.

JAY
Let's get round to the house on Greenwold street.

GAL
No fucking way. You're going home to have a nice little lie down.

JAY
Drop me off then. I'll go on foot.

GAL
The fuck I will.

JAY
There is no way I'm leaving.

GAL
We're going off list here - big time. I don't know what the fuck Shel will say.

JAY
Then don't tell her.

GAL looks away. He shakes his head.

EXT. GREENWOLD STREET HOUSE - DUSK.

GAL and JAY pull up in front of a 70s council house. There's a light on in the kitchen.

INT. HIT CAR NO. 2 - DUSK.

GAL looks over to JAY.

GAL
Don't hang about.

JAY
If I'm not out in twenty minutes come and get me.

GAL
Don't worry, I will.

JAY cocks his pistol, tucks it in his trousers and leaves the car. GAL watches anxiously as his friend crosses the road. He knows it's a mistake, but he's powerless. JAY disappears around the side of the house.

INT. HIT CAR NO. 2 - DUSK.

GAL checks his watch and drinks a carton of orange juice.

INT. HIT CAR NO. 2 - DUSK.

GAL checks his watch again. He looks over at the house just as a man walks past with his dog. The man waves to GAL. GAL shakes his head miserably.

INT. HIT CAR NO. 2 - DUSK.

GAL cocks his gun, gets out of the car and makes his way over to the house.

EXT. GREENWOLD STREET - DUSK.

GAL edges along the side of the house. The back door is open. Light spills out. GAL enters the kitchen to find a kettle whistling on the hob and a dead dog in

the middle of the floor. Blood seeps between the tiles. GAL hears banging. Rhythmic. Workman-like. It's coming from the lower ground floor. Steep stairs take GAL down to JAY's level.
A dead man is slumped in a corner. In another, JAY is busy smashing a man's head against the wall. There is a video camera on a tripod and a bed in the corner. JAY looks round as GAL approaches. He drops the man unceremoniously. His face is pummeled flat, but a smile is still discernible.

JAY
That time already?

GAL is grim, sober.

GAL
We have to go.

JAY
Fine.

EXT. DUAL CARRIAGE WAY - NIGHT.

GAL drives carefully. Both hands on the steering wheel looking straight ahead. The heaviness of the atmosphere is reflected in the accompanying music.

INT. HIT CAR NO. 2 - NIGHT.

GAL
You're covered in blood.
JAY
I'll burn them.

GAL
You know what they say is the sign of a good painter and decorator?

JAY
What.

GAL
Clean overalls. No bodging.

JAY
Point taken.

EXT. PETROL STATION. - NIGHT.

The car pulls into the forecourt. GAL buys bottled water.

EXT. SIDE STREET. - NIGHT.

JAY slowly, methodically washes his hands, fore-arms and face over the gutter as GAL counts cash in the car. He stops for a moment to observe JAY in the mirror. His thoughts are speculative and sus-pect… his faith in JAY left back in that basement on Greenwold street.
GAL looks at the money and then back at JAY.

EXT. WASTE LAND - NIGHT.

GAL and JAY burn bodies and drink lagers. Cinders dance in the humid air. They stand apart, engrossed in their own thoughts for a moment.

JAY
It doesn't feel wrong.

GAL
That's good.

JAY
They're bad people.

GAL
That's why they're on the list.

JAY
They should suffer.

GAL
No question.

JAY
But they don't seem to. Not enough anyway.

GAL
You do a thorough job.

JAY
I try to beat it out of them. You know… remorse… fear. But they don't seem to understand my position. You find that?

GAL
Come on. Let's go home.

EXT. MOTORWAY - NIGHT.

JAY drives, GAL snores. The maroon Mondeo looms in the rear-view mirror. He nudges GAL but GAL doesn't respond. JAY exits the motorway, slipping into rural darkness and winding country roads.

EXT. COUNTRY LANE - NIGHT.

JAY picks up speed. When there is sufficient distance between himself and the maroon Mondeo, he pulls off road and kills the head lights.
He waits and watches for the maroon Mondeo, which drives past at speed.
After a time JAY backs the car out of the field and back onto the road.

INT. HOTEL NO. 3 - NIGHT.

JAY showers and prepares himself for another fitful night of sleep. He turns the blanket down and the lights off. The distant yellow glow of motorway traffic draws him to the window. Barren scrubland stretches as far as the eye can see.
FIONA, alone, possessionless, stands amongst the grass. For a moment JAY feel like no one else ex-

ists. FIONA waves languidly. JAY waves back.

INT. JAY'S HOUSE - DUSK.

JAY bowls through the front door dropping shopping bags and smiles. He's oddly nervous and watches GAL drive off with mild regret. SHEL appears with a questioning expression.

SHEL
I didn't expect you back... There's nothing to eat.

JAY
We'll go out.

SHEL
It's a school night. What happened?

JAY
I just want to see Sammy.

SHEL
He's got a play date. We'll talk about it later.

FIONA appears from the kitchen.

FIONA
Hi, Jay, you back?

SHEL
We were just having a glass of wine.

FIONA
And a moan. Should I go?

SHEL
Don't be silly... you were here first.

INT. JAY'S HOUSE. BEDROOM - DUSK.

JAY sits on the bed listening to FIONA's long good-bye. SHEL closes the front door and is soon standing over him, cradling his head as he cries.

SHEL
Its alright. Whatever it is, we'll sort it. It's alright.

INT. JAY'S HOUSE. CHILD'S BEDROOM - NIGHT.

JAY watches SAM sleep buried in cuddly toys.

INT. JAY'S HOUSE. SITTING ROOM - MORNING.

SAM is going rummaging through JAY's bag.

JAY
Don't touch that stuff, it's dirty.

SAM
This one looks like you.

SAM holds up the picture of the knight JAY and GAL saved from the first kill.

INT. JAY'S HOUSE. BATHROOM - DAY.

Starting at the soiled bandage wrapped around his cut hand, JAY follows the angry rash that now runs the length of his arm.

JAY
Shel!

SHEL sticks her head around the door. For the first time JAY realizes how bad his arm is.

SHEL
Jesus, Jay!

JAY
You think it's bad?

SHEL
Just a bit. What the fuck happened!

JAY
I don't know.

SHEL
Let me have a look.

SHEL takes JAY's hand and unwraps the bandage carefully.

JAY
Leave it.

SHEL
Don't be stupid.

She backs away from the smell.

SHEL
It's infected. You have to see the doctor.

JAY
I'm not going.

INT. DOCTOR'S SURGERY - DAY.

THE DOCTOR sits as far as possible from JAY, observing him with scepticism and the usual lack of empathy.

DOCTOR
Would you say you were suffering from stress?

JAY
Yes.

DOCTOR
Interrupted sleep?

JAY
Yes.

DOCTOR
Fatigue? Nausea?

JAY
Yes. No.

There is a long awkward moment in which JAY expects to be examined but isn't.

DOCTOR
You're fine.

JAY
I know. But my hand isn't. Are you going to look at it?

DOCTOR
Better still, I can give you some advice.

JAY
What happened to Dr. Bapkin?

DOCTOR
The past is gone and the future is not yet here. There is only ever this moment.

JAY
Okay.

DOCTOR
Good.

THE DOCTOR smiles. JAY leaves.

INT. GAL'S HOUSE. SITTING ROOM - NIGHT.

GAL sits on the floor of his sitting room surrounded by photos and beer cans. We see shots of the desecrated tomb of a medieval knight, THE PRIEST's house, and himself and JAY on surveillance.
GAL opens another folder marked 'Kiev' and winces.

INT. JAY'S HOUSE - MORNING.

JAY necks three pills and rubs his temples. He feels dislocated as he watches SAM play on the carpet in front of the television.

SHEL
JAYYYYY!

JAY heaves himself up from the sofa and follows SHEL's alarm into the garden.
Lulu the cat has been tied to a stake in the middle of the lawn. Her fur is matted with blood and her teeth are tied around her head.

INT. JAY'S HOUSE. KITCHEN - MORNING.

JAY stands frozen in front of the kitchen window. The sink is full of dirty dishes, and the table is in disarray. SHEL comes up behind him and puts her arms around JAY's neck. They both peer at their own images reflected in the black glass.

SHEL
Poor Lulu.

JAY
Why would they kill a helpless cat?

SHEL
Maybe kids.

JAY
What kind of sick bastard would do that?

INT. JAY'S HOUSE. HALLWAY - MORNING.

SHEL answers the door. GAL knows her well and immediately registers the look of concern on her face.

GAL
What's up sweetheart?

SHEL
Someone's murdered the cat.

JAY appears behind SHEL.

INT. JAY'S HOUSE. GARAGE - MORNING.

The two men stand solemnly over the cat's corpse.

JAY
I fucking loved that cat.

GAL
I didn't know.

JAY
Neither did I until it happened.

GAL
Look…

JAY
What.

GAL
It's a message isn't it.

JAY
Received loud and clear.

GAL
With the money we picked up we could sack the rest of the job off.

JAY
What?

GAL
There are pictures of us outside the priest's house, Jay. There's a file on Kiev. How the fuck did they get that?

JAY
So.

GAL
We have to pack this one in. It's bad for your health… and mine.

JAY
If I start something, I finish it.

GAL
Where does it finish? That's my point.

JAY
You don't have the taste for it any-more.

GAL
I just can't work with you if you're going to go over the top every time you get a lump hammer in your hand.

JAY
Look, I'm sorry. What more can I say.

GAL
That we can go to the client and sound him out about replacements.

JAY
I'm going to bury the cat.

JAY grabs up a shoe box, the cat's corpse and a shovel, and stomps off into the garden.

INT. JAY'S HOUSE. KITCHEN - MORNING.

GAL and SHEL stand at the window watching JAY bury the cat with full honours. SAM stands by his dad trying to be brave.

SHEL
What's going on, Gal?

GAL
I don't fucking know but it's not good.

SHEL
I thought that if I ignored it, it might just go away.

GAL
It hasn't.

SHEL
I can't let him have any more time off. He needs to be working. Too much thinking makes him crazy.

GAL
Well I'm done.

SHEL
What?

GAL
It doesn't feel right anymore. I can't read him.

SHEL unexpectedly grabs GAL. Her embrace is tender and intimate. Its flirtatiousness embarrasses GAL. He flushes. He's robbed of his usual bravado.

SHEL
You can't say that.

GAL
I'll see this job through, but-

SHEL
Gal. You're my soldier. I need you. I can't cope alone. It takes both of us to deal with him. Without you I'd drown.

GAL
Well, I'll see.

SHEL
All this talk about Jay. What about you? You don't get enough attention, and that's my fault, not Jay's. I'm the one you should be punishing.

GAL grins from ear to ear.

EXT. JAY'S HOUSE. GARDEN - MORNING.

JAY looks at SHEL and GAL.

INT. JAY'S HOUSE. KITCHEN - MORNING.

The doorbell rings. SHEL releases GAL and goes to answer it. SHEL comes back into the kitchen followed by a sheepish FIONA.

FIONA
Hi Gal, fancy seeing you here.

INT. JAY'S HOUSE - AFTERNOON.

JAY comes in through the back door. He's covered in mud, his sleeved rolled up. SAM is filthy, but they both look contented.

JAY
Where is everyone?

SHEL
Gone. More important, where have you been? One minute you were in the garden and the next-

JAY
We went for a walk to look for foxes, didn't we, mate?

SAM
Daddy said I could have a puppy.

SHEL
Did he?

JAY
We're going to call it Arthur.

SHEL
What if it's a girl?

JAY
Gwinny?

SHEL
Go upstairs and take those dirties off.
We'll have a bath in a minute.

SAM runs off upstairs.

JAY
I don't want to talk about it.

SHEL
Well he's ready to pack it in.

JAY
Maybe he should. He's gone soft.

SHEL slaps JAY across the face. He looks genuinely shocked. So does she.

SHEL
Wake up.

INT. JAY'S HOUSE. BEDROOM - DAY.

JAY, sprawled out on top of the bed, wakes with a sudden jolt. SHEL bends over him.

SHEL
Jay?

SHEL smiles and holds a large tumbler of whiskey out to him.

SHEL
Sorry.

JAY
Me too.

SHEL
Do you think if you get replacements they will let you go free of the contract?

JAY
I don't know. Is that what you want?

SHEL
It doesn't look good, but if we are compromised here…

INT. HOTEL NO. 1 - DUSK.

THE CLIENT is standing with two large men.

CLIENT
A man can't change.

GAL
We can get you top-drawer replacements. They even look like us.

CLIENT
It is your job. The job is you. You have been picked.

GAL
And if we say fuck you very much and good night?

CLIENT
Then you die. And your families, they die. You touch me, you die, your families die.

GAL
There's no wriggle room on that?

CLIENT
No.

THE CLIENT throws money on the table and a new list. JAY appears amused.

JAY
Another?

THE CLIENT smiles at JAY.

GAL
How long have we been working for you?

CLIENT
Please, don't embarrass yourself. I like you. I see you. What you are.

JAY
What are we?

CLIENT
Cogs.

GAL
In what? What is this?

CLIENT
You are helping with the reconstruction. The money is the oil. You would soon find that without it you would seize up. So, keep turning. It's simple.

THE CLIENT leaves the room. The two large threatening men remain.

GAL
What reconstruction?

GAL goes to follow THE CLIENT and scuffles with the men.

INT. HIT CAR NO. 3 - DUSK.

JAY and GAL sit.

JAY
Well that went well.

GAL
Don't say it.

JAY
I'm not saying anything, You're the one who's getting cold feet.

GAL
We've been played.

JAY
Have we? I just think your expectations have changed.

GAL
What about you?

JAY
What about me?

INT. JAY'S HOUSE - NIGHT.

JAY lets himself in quietly, thinking not to wake SHEL and SAM, but finds SHEL packing cases and checking lists.

JAY
What's this?

SHEL
I'm leaving.

JAY
What?

SHEL
I'm going to the safe house with Sam, just till this job's over, then we'll have to sit down and have a serious talk about your professional working practice.

JAY
Hang on… what fucking safe house?

SHEL
Just somewhere I keep on standby. I'll skype you when we get there.

JAY
Where the fuck is it? I'll drive you.

SHEL
You don't need to know right now.

JAY
What?

SHEL
Jay. You're in serious danger of losing all of this. Is that what you want?

JAY
No.

SHEL
Then sort it out.

EXT. JAY'S HOUSE - NIGHT.

JAY carries his sleeping son to the car. He tenderly straps SAM in as SHEL packs the last of her stuff, gets in behind the wheel and drives away without looking back.

INT. JAY'S HOUSE - DAY.

A photo is on the kitchen table and a name. GAL taps away on his Blackberry.

GAL
He's an MP.

JAY
More acceptable than a priest?

GAL
I can't say it's not a relief.

JAY
His name's on the list, that's all we need to know.

GAL
Okay.

JAY
Sure? Not going to go crying to Shel?

GAL
I might if I could reach her.

JAY
She's having a little holiday.

GAL
She didn't mention anything.

JAY
She's my wife, not yours.

GAL
Just as long as you treat her like one and not a fucking door mat.

JAY
You're the last man I need to take lessons in love from.

GAL slaps JAY round the face.

JAY
What the fuck what that?

GAL
A bitch slap. I'm not your fucking minion. I'm my own man.

JAY
Oh yeah.

JAY punches GAL in the stomach. They roll about on the floor fighting. GAL gets on top and starts punching JAY.

JAY
Don't touch the face.

The fight is a bit pathetic and not the Bourne-style punch up you'd expect, but it's wholehearted and sincere. Their frustration and irritation with each other is clear.

INT. KITCHEN - DAY.

GAL and JAY crack open beers. JAY holds his to his cheek to dull the ache. They both sit looking at one of SHEL's ornaments, now smashed into pieces - a victim of war.

JAY
I'm telling Shel you started it.

GAL
She thinks I'm a saint.

JAY
She doesn't know you.

GAL
I'll get another one. She won't notice.

JAY
She notices everything.

GAL
Yeah.

GAL absently tries to fit the broken bits of pottery together.

GAL
I can't stop thinking about Fiona.

JAY
Yeah?

GAL
I think it might be love.

JAY
You hardly know her!

GAL
Sometimes these things happen.

JAY
She gaffer-taped your cock.

GAL
I've marked that down as an erotic cry for help.

JAY
I can't remember what I was like before Shel.

GAL
Fucking lonely, no doubt, like me.

JAY
They say there's someone for everyone.

GAL
It's not much to ask is it?
(PAUSE.)

JAY
Let's go and kill this MP then

GAL
Yeah. Nice

EXT. MOTORWAY - DAY.

JAY and GAL drive down the motorway.

INT. HIT CAR NO. 3 - DAY.

JAY and GAL are driving through villages and past large houses.

EXT. WOODS - DUSK.

The car heads off road. JAY jumps out and cuts a

chain on a gate. He pushes it back and GAL drives the car through. JAY puts the gate back. He gets back in the car. They drive on.

EXT. BEACH - DUSK.

The car pulls up at a beach. JAY and GAL pull on their outdoor gear and cover the vehicle with camo net.
JAY phones SHEL.

JAY
Love? Everything fine here. I don't know how you think of all this shit. Look, I know I've been a berk, but it will be cleared up in a day or so. Promise. And then we can talk to the builders together about the conservatory, O.K? Good. Love you. Love to Sammy.

They walk towards chalk cliffs.
A weathered smugglers' doorway appears out of the gloom. They jimmy it open and crawl inside.

INT. TUNNEL - DUSK.

GAL and JAY trudge through a tunnel weighed down by equipment. It's pitch black. They illuminate it with torches.

EXT. WOODS - DUSK.

The two men crawl out of a hatch into a wood. They drag their bags.

EXT. WOODS - DUSK.

GAL and JAY cross woodland to the edge of the es-tate.
GAL screws together a rifle with a night scope.

JAY
The air's good.

GAL
We should do this more often.

JAY
Kill rich people?

GAL
No, get out in the fresh air.

JAY
Like big game hunters on the Serengeti.

GAL
I like that. It sounds heroic.

JAY
Up here I reckon.

GAL
Okay.

They move forwards through the thick bracken.

EXT WOODS - DAY.

JAY and GAL have their shovels out and they are digging into the earth.

EXT. WOODS - DUSK.

JAY and GAL have built themselves a hide. GAL opens up a bag and gets a fire going. He brews tea. JAY returns from a wander with a dead rabbit.

JAY
Dinner's on me.

GAL
Where did you get that?

JAY
They're everywhere if you know where to look.

GAL
Tea?

JAY
Lovely.

EXT. WOODS - DUSK.

JAY cooks the rabbit. GAL watches the fire.

GAL
You look right at home.

JAY
You were right.

GAL
About what?

JAY
Being out here. I'd almost forgotten what it's like to be me.

GAL
The two musketeers!

JAY
We'll go and have a look at his gaff tomorrow.

GAL
Listen to that.

JAY
What?

GAL
Nothing. No traffic.

JAY
Yeah. It's perfect. As long as we don't get picked off by some yokel farmer with a blunderbuss.

GAL
What's the plan?

JAY
I can't be bothered with anything flash.

GAL
What? Not march him into the middle of the village square and chop his head off with an axe?
(PAUSE.)

JAY
Who's in the house?

GAL
He's a bachelor. Why don't you ever read the brief?

JAY
You don't keep a dog and bark yourself, do you?

GAL grabs JAY and gives him a good playful shake around the neck.

GAL
See? See? My old mate's still in there!
(INTO JAY'S EAR…)
Hello, hello? Is there anyone home?

JAY becomes suddenly serious.

JAY
Let's leave it till two or three. Let it settle down. Look at the layout of the house.

EXT. FIELDS - NIGHT.

JAY and GAL lay on their bellies in open, manicured, more pastoral landscape. In the distance is a large illuminated manor house. JAY looks through his binoculars at its massive conservatory.

JAY
Now that's what I call a fucking conservatory!

GAL
Let's have a look.

GAL grabs the glasses and looks.

JAY
Thank fuck Shel's not here. I'd never hear the end of it.

GAL
It's not right.

JAY
What?

GAL
That one man lives in all that alone.

JAY
None of it is. That's why we're here.

GAL
Come on, lets bed down, he's probably fucking the scullery maid.

INT. HIDE - NIGHT.

JAY and GAL lay like sardines in their sleeping bags. Their heads stick out the end of the hide. They look up at the stars and tree top and pass a joint between each other.

GAL
It's a generational thing, isn't it? I might be able to drag myself out of the shit and get a house. My son will think it's normal to have a gaff. Maybe down the road, his son might be a doctor or something. Slowly the family drags itself towards respectability.

JAY
You reckon? I think my family have been doing this job for generations. A long line of hatchet men. You know?

GAL
That's kind of depressing.

JAY
Is it? Makes me feel proud. I like to think of my poor hairy-arsed relation, two hundred years ago - dipping arrows in shit and firing them at Frenchmen. Or sticking long knives into a knight's armor. Gives me a warm feeling.

GAL
I guess.

JAY
Look at yourself. You're built for this. It's genetics, innit?

GAL
Didn't your old man work for the council?

JAY
Yeah.

INT. HIDE - NIGHT.

JAY
Gal, you awake?

GAL
I wasn't but I am now.

JAY
I'm sorry about all that business.

GAL
I know.

JAY
I don't know where it comes from.

GAL
You're a fucking madman, but you are my mate. So let's leave it at that.

JAY
Once we get out of this, we should really become salesmen.

GAL is suddenly excited. He leans up on his elbow.

GAL
What? Doggy charms? Miniature manicure kits?

JAY
I was thinking more M14's and sub-machine guns.

GAL is slightly deflated.

GAL
Maybe.

JAY
Reckon we could be good at it.

GAL
You know what my dream job would be?

JAY
What, this isn't it!

GAL
Boxercise.

They both laugh.

JAY
Fuck off.

GAL
I mean it. I think it's got the potential to do real good in the world.

INT. HIDE - NIGHT.

JAY wakes. GAL snores. JAY listens intently to the eerie sound of pipe music carried on the wind through the woods.
He crawls out of the hide. In the distance he can see the flickering light of a burning torch.

EXT. WOODS - NIGHT.

A distant, low chant is carried to JAY and GAL on the gentle breeze.

JAY
What the fuck's that?

GAL scrambles groggily through the hide opening.

GAL
What?

JAY
Can't you hear it?

GAL
I can't hear anything, mate. How much more of that shit did you smoke?

JAY
Listen.

GAL
Nothing.

The sound grows louder. Lights flicker amongst foliage. GAL and JAY stay stock still.
Torches moving through the woods. As they approach it becomes clear that they are held aloft by naked men and women wearing masks woven from corn.
Others follow dressed in white, like a flock of excited brides and grooms.
At the front of the procession is the MP and an old man, both leading a young woman by the hands. She also is dressed in white, but her gown is covered in

banknotes that rustle in the wind like feathers. She is proceeded by a sort of maid-of-honour who scatters bank notes in her path.
JAY and GAL are mute with astonishment.
The naked men and women sing now. There are about thirty of them.
GAL and JAY follow the procession through estate land, crawling on their bellies and picking up fallen bank notes as they go.
JAY and GAL move carefully under cover.
GAL rubs his forehead. His head aches and his nose bleeds heavily.

GAL
Mother of God.

EXT. WOODS - NIGHT.

The group are chanting and singing with greater intent now. The MP throws a rope over a tree and secures it firmly, while the old man embraces the bride warmly before stepping back. The bride walks forwards alone. All other participants back away respectfully.
The bride climbs onto a stool, puts her neck into the noose and waves.

GAL
We have to stop this.

In that split second the bride hangs herself.
There is silence as her legs thrash wildly.
JAY's eyes fill with tears.
The old man, who had jointly led the girl to her death, steps forwards and ceremoniously receives a pile of money.
People dance and cheer wildly. The sound of champagne corks popping and glasses clinking as the girl swings in the wind.
GAL throws up.
JAY aims the rifle at the MP. GAL grabs JAY's shoulder.

GAL
Don't, there's too many.

JAY fires. He misses and a man standing next to the MP falls in a puff of blood. The MP turns. It's almost that he can see where the gunfire has come from. But he doesn't run. He opens his arms out as if welcoming his own death. JAY fires again and hits the MP in the chest. The MP falls back and the other people look over to where JAY and GAL are.

JAY
I'm going to thin them out a bit.

JAY fires until he runs out of bullets. Naked people drop left and right.
There is the sound of shotguns being fired back.
The rest of the people start running towards them.

GAL
We've got to go…

The marchers turn on them and chase them through the woods. It's chaotic. You'd think the marchers' natural instinct would be to run from the gunfire, but they seem drawn to it instead.

EXT. WOODS - NIGHT.

GAL and JAY are running for their lives. The woods behind them are alight with flares and flames. People shouting and dogs barking.
GAL and JAY catch their breath by a tree.
They make off again. Running towards the smugglers' tunnel.
JAY and GAL crawl down to the opening to the tunnel.
The processional participants are nearby.
JAY and GAL slosh through the tunnel.

INT. SMUGGLERS TUNNEL - NIGHT.

GAL and JAY run along the smugglers' tunnel as best they can. It's back-breaking work, crouched over in the freezing darkness. They hear a crash as marchers drop into the tunnel in pursuit. Flickering torches close in on them.

GAL returns fire with his pistol. A figure falls into the water. GAL fires around the corner.
JAY, having progressed slightly ahead, loses sight of GAL.

JAY
Gal!

He hears screams from GAL.
He fires down the tunnel

JAY
GAL!

There's nothing. He looks back.

JAY
Fuck.

INT. TUNNEL - NIGHT.

GAL is stabbed repeatedly and slowly.

GAL
No. No. No.

The stabbing seems endless.
GAL turns and crawls down the tunnel, but they follow still jabbing him with knives and pulling at his intestines.
GAL pulls out a pistol and shoots two of them.
They grab at his intestines and pull some more. GAL staggers, falls, trailing guts.
JAY follows the echoing noises.

JAY
Gal?

He moves through the tunnel and finds GAL fighting feebly. JAY shoots GAL's opponents.

JAY
Let's get you out of here, mate.

JAY drags GAL through the tunnel. In the distance more figures close in.
JAY fires down the tunnel.

GAL
I can't get up. They've cut my hamstrings.

JAY
We've got to go.

GAL
I'm done.

JAY
Fuck.

GAL
Tell Shel I'm sorry.

JAY
Gal.

GAL
Do it.

JAY kisses GAL on the forehead. GAL smiles.

GAL
Sorry. Thank you.

JAY shoots GAL in the head. He slumps to the floor.

EXT. BEACH - NIGHT.

JAY runs out of the rocks and scrambles towards his car.

EXT. BEACH - NIGHT.

JAY drives off. On the back of the vehicle we see a mark in blood. The same mark that FIONA carved into JAY's bathroom cabinet that first night at dinner.

INT. HIT CAR NO. 3 - NIGHT.

JAY pulls over and throws up. He unwraps his wounded hand and digs into it with a knife.

INT. HIT CAR NO. 3 - NIGHT.

JAY is driving up the motorway. His vision is blurred. Things move in slow motion around him but his mind spins out of control.

EXT. WOODS NEAR COTTAGE - NIGHT.

JAY drives up to the cottage. He gets out and walks in.

INT. COTTAGE - NIGHT.

SHEL is sitting at the table. She has a glass of wine by her. She looks up angrily.

JAY
It's over.

SHEL
Where's Gal?

JAY
Gal's gone.

SHEL
Gone? What do you mean? Gone.

JAY sits at the table with his head in his hands. He sobs. SAM comes out.

SAM
Daddy! Can we go home now? What's the matter with Daddy? Is he sick?

SHEL
Don't worry, baby. Your Dad's just tired.

JAY
Hey, son. How's it going?

SAM
I don't like it. It's quiet but noisy with birds pecking and the black's too black. We saw a dead mole on a fence.

JAY
It's just different.

SHEL
You go to bed honey.

INT. COTTAGE - NIGHT.

SHEL is drinking. JAY is looking out the window.

SHEL
Sit down.

JAY
Shhh.

SHEL
What?

JAY
Something.

JAY pulls out a pistol from his overnight bag.
He opens the front door and creeps outside. He edges around the house. It's very dark. He creeps - heart in mouth. He makes a circle of the cottage. He doesn't see anything. He gets back to the front door. On the door is a dead fox. It's head has been skinned.

JAY looks shocked. He takes down the fox and throws it into the bushes. He goes over to his car. He sees the tires have been slashed.
He goes back into the house.

SHEL
Let's go home now.

JAY
We're not going anywhere. They've slashed the tires.

SHEL
Fuck. How many guns have you got?

JAY
A rifle and a pistol.

Suddenly, outside, dozens of torches are lit. JAY runs to the window. The torches are beyond the hedgerow.
JAY opens the door and fires in the direction of the torches.
He fires until his pistol is empty. He reloads.
There's silence. SAM has woken up. He comes out of his bedroom and his mother holds him.

SAM
It's too noisy!

SHEL
Just fireworks.

JAY goes outside. The torches are on poles. Nobody there.
He runs back inside to the house.

JAY
It's bullshit.

SHEL
What?

JAY
I don't think there are many… They would have attacked.

SHEL
They expect us to hide here and wait to die.

JAY
I am going out there to find them.

SHEL takes a gun, racks it and puts it in her belt.

SHEL
Let them come.

They kiss.

JAY gets up and sneaks over to the fuse box. He pulls the fuses and the cottage goes into darkness.

JAY
I love you.

He goes over to the back window and sneaks out of the cottage.

EXT. SAFE HOUSE. WOODS - NIGHT.

JAY moves through the undergrowth, rifle at his chest, heart in his mouth.
The night is weighed down by silence.
JAY moves along a hedge and ducks down into more undergrowth.
JAY is inside the hedge.
JAY slithers into a ditch and moves through stagnant water. He sees feet moving through the branches. He holds his breath. Their whispering reaches him, but he can't quite make out what is being said.

INT. SAFE HOUSE - NIGHT.

SHEL sits frozen in darkness, listening to every sound intently. She hears cloth against cloth. Boots creaking on tarmac. The sounds of her silencer screwing onto her pistol.
She releases the safety on her pistol and crouches down.
There's a straining noise as the door is popped open.
A figure enters the room. Another behind.
SHEL holds the pistol up and fires.
The first figure falls, then the second.
Bullet casings roll on the wooden floor.

SHEL rushes, shooting another figure cloaked in darkness by the hedgerow, who also falls with a thud.
She re-enters the cottage, drawn by faint moans.
She shoots the second figure as he lays on the ground and returns to the first to finish him off.
She is breathing heavily.

SHEL
(IN SWEDISH.)
<Useless fuckers>

SHEL reloads her pistol. She hears another noise.
She crouches down.

EXT. SAFE HOUSE. WOODS - NIGHT.

JAY moves towards voices. He is in the woods now. He sees figures moving about. He crouches beside a tree and clicks off the safety on the rifle.
He moves through the undergrowth. In a clearing he can see some people. He can see a figure.
He aims the rifle. He has a masked man in his sights.
He moves to squeeze the trigger.
Suddenly he is hit with a pickaxe handle.

EXT. DEEPER WOODS - NIGHT.

JAY opens his eyes. He can see the ground. He's tied up.
He rolls onto his side.
Two black-clad guards grab him and pull him forward.
Also present are the HIGH PRIEST and the NAKED WOMAN with the thorn blindfold.

PRIEST
You and your family will die.

JAY
No.

PRIEST
There is only one way you can redeem yourself. You must take *our* list. Then you will be free.

JAY
Okay… Okay…

THORN WOMAN gives JAY the list.

PRIEST
The first person on the list is the hunchback. We want you to prove your loyalty to us by killing the hunchback.

They take JAY's hand and THE PRIEST cuts it. The blood runs across the list. The list has fifty names on it.
JAY is dragged to his feet and marched through the woods. Torches flicker lighting up the tree tops.

EXT. DEEPER WOODS. THE CULT CIRCLE - NIGHT.

Masked faces jeer at him.
In a clearing there is a circle of worshippers holding torches. JAY is thrown into the circle. He has his shirt stripped off him and a mask strapped hard to his face.
A worshipper thrusts a knife into his hand. He looks wildly around.
The circle opens and another masked figure staggers in. The figure is a hunchback, holding a knife.
The hunchback staggers forward.
JAY moves towards the hunchback brandishing his knife.
The hunchback starts stabbing at JAY. Slashing madly from side to side. It cuts JAY's arm. JAY jumps back - the torchbearers push him back towards the hunchback.
JAY grabs the hunchback and attacks it in a frenzy, stabbing it in the chest and back.
The hunchback falls to the ground, mortally wounded.
JAY experiences a moment of exhilaration.
He pulls the mask off to reveal SHEL - pained, twisted features.
She laughs at him as she bleeds to death.
JAY pulls back the hunchback to see SAM strapped to her back.
The others take their masks off. THE DOCTOR, THE CLIENT, FIONA.

FIONA steps forwards and holds JAY's hand. She slips a crown on his head.
The others come forwards and each in turn shakes his hand.

WOMAN
Open your eyes. You're awake.

EXT. WOODS - DAWN.

JAY wakes with a fevered start next to the bodies of SHEL and SAM.
In his hand, a piece of blood-soaked paper.

Title:

The Kill List

JAY gets up and walks away.

EXT. WOODS - DAWN.

He walks towards a car.
FIONA is waiting for him.
She smiles.
He gets in.
They drive away.

THE END

A FIELD IN ENGLAND

EXT. HEDGEROW - DAY.

The camera follows the course of a dense hedgerow along the edge of a fallow field, left to right.

The sky is grey and low. Mud and shit predominate.

Muzzle smoke drifts across from a battle in the field on the far, unseen, side of the hedge.

The sounds of chaos accompany it: Officers screaming, mortally injured men whimpering, horses whinnying, impact, explosion, death.

CUTLER VOICE.OVER
(DESPERATE/ INSISTENT.)
Friend?

We come upon two men, CUTLER and FRIEND.

(CUTLER: A civilian. A rough type who has accumulated several extra weapons, suggesting he is a plunderer.)

(FRIEND: A foot soldier.)

Friend is fatally injured. Cutler shakes him vigorously, trying to revive him.

CUTLER
(STRESSED.)
Hey. Friend. You're name? Give me your name.

Friend appears to die.

His head drops back, his eyes close, his mouth falls open, slack-jawed.

CUTLER
(TO HIMSELF.)
Fuck.

Cutler drops Friend unceremoniously.

Cutler measures his feet against Friend's ragged shoes and decides against steeling them.

TROWER V.O
(SOME WAY OFF/ ROARING.)
Whiteheeeeaaaad!

Cutler looks over his shoulder down the length of the hedgerow.

CUT TO:

WE SEE Trower's enraged screaming face at close quarters.

(TROWER: A down-at-heel gentleman. Roguish, violently self-righteous.)

TROWER
(ROARING.)
Where are you, man!

EXT. HEDGEROW - DAY.

WHITEHEAD, is pulling himself through the hedgerow with difficulty.

WHITEHEAD
(MUMBLING DESPERATELY.)
Please, Merciful God, don't let him find me.

(WHITEHEAD: An assistant to an Astrologer and Alchemist. A self-respecting man who has battled to stay neat and tidy in extreme conditions, but who is now weary and disillusioned.)

CUT TO:

Cutler is stealing Friend's humble CLAY PIPE from his pocket.

TROWER V.O
Six months!

Cutler ducks down as TROWER passes on the other side of the hedge atop a skittish horse, left to right.

CUT TO:

Trower rants at the air around him.

TROWER
To root out one Irishman.

CUT TO:

Whitehead in the hedgerow, cowering.

WHITEHEAD
(MUMBLING DESPERATELY.)
Rid me of that pompous arse.

CUT TO:

Trower over the hedgerow.

TROWER
Six months, Whitehead!

CUT TO:

Cutler making his way along the hedgerow towards Whitehead.

TROWER V.O(CONT'D)
Instead what do you find?

CUT TO:

Whitehead extracts himself from the hedgerow and slumps against it.

TROWER V.O (CONT'D)
The enemy!

CUT TO:

Whitehead puts his hands together in prayer and closes his eyes.

WHITEHEAD
(MUMBLING DESPERATELY.)
Please hear me.

TROWER V.O
I care not what the Master might say.

CUT TO:

Trower hits the hedgerow with violent frustration.

TROWER
No more mummery!

CUT TO:

Cutler crawling closer to Whitehead.

TROWER V.O
You're finished scrivener, you hear me?
You'll make a better scarecrow.

CUT TO:

Trower is now directly above Whitehead across the hedge looking about but does not detect Whitehead.

TROWER
I shall hang you from the nearest tree, see if I don't!

Cutler taps Whitehead on the shoulder.

CUTLER
(AUDIBLE TO TROWER.)
Hey. Friend.

Whitehead flinches, opens his eyes and looks at Cutler with terror.

Whitehead screeches like an abused milkmaid.

WHITEHEAD
Argghh!

Trower leans over the hedge and sees the two crouching men.

Trower's expression turns from one of abject fury to triumphant, vengeful satisfaction.

TROWER
There you are, you coward!

Whitehead looks up at Trower like a kicked dog.

WHITEHEAD
This is the place. I am certain this time. He is here!

TROWER
Lies!

WHITEHEAD
Astrology cannot be an exact business if the particulars of the questions asked are ill-defined, or the individual sort is-

TROWER
Damn your impudence, you obsequious little turd!

Trower is unceremoniously piked through back.

WHITEHEAD
Oh my God!

Trower contorts.

TROWER
Argghhhh!

The pike snaps, (retaining approximately five foot of wooden pole).

Trower is dismounted by the impaling but refuses to die straight off.

He scrambles through the hedge, raging and grabbing at Whitehead.

TROWER
Nolens volens. Your privy parts are doomed, Homunculus!

Whitehead scrambles back away from Trower, hands still locked in prayer.

TROWER
Come here!

WHITEHEAD
No thank you!

Cutler finishes Trower off with a perfunctory shot from his own weapon.

Trower runs out of life halfway through the hedge.

TROWER
(HISSING.)
Bawd's Baaasssstaarrrd.

His outstretched arm and pointing finger are the only parts fully emerged from the hedge on Cutler and Whitehead's side.

There is a moment of stillness shared by Whitehead, Cutler and Trower's corpse.

Cutler puts his finger on the spike of the pike head, sticking out through Trower's chest.

Cutler raises an eyebrow at Whitehead.

CUTLER
Looks like your prayer is answered.

Whitehead looks back down at his own hands still clasped in prayer.

Whitehead looks along Trower's lacerated arm. Along Trower's gold-ringed finger. Out into the field to which it clearly points.

(Whitehead's POV of the field - A strange manifestation)

CUTLER
What do you see, friend?

CUT TO:

Cutler looks at Whitehead's squinting expression and then out into the empty field.

Cutler sees nothing.

Whitehead shakes his head, nothing.

WHITEHEAD
(SANGUINE.)
Nothing, perhaps. Perhaps he is right. Only shadows.

EXT. FIELD - DAY.

Title sequence:

Music/ drumming (see 'The Call' from The Six Calls to War)

(Image of the camera circling the field at a low level through the grass at speed. Possibly in colour. Something more illustrative of the magic of the field. Or done as a wood cut, like in a pamphlet. Or… the entire film speeded up and condensed into a very short space of time.)

Title:

A Field in England.

Credits.

CUT TO:

EXT. HEDGEROW - DAY.

There is a sudden explosion from the other side of the hedge.

Caption:

Welsh English border.

1648.

Earth rains down on Whitehead and Cutler.

Whitehead collapses to the floor and grasps his ears.

We hear a high-pitched ringing.

Whitehead looks up as Cutler.

CUT TO:

Cutler has his foot on Trower's chest, pulling the pike through his body.

Cutler turns to find Whitehead watching him in horror.

Cutler says something inaudible to Whitehead.

Whitehead shakes his head, indicating he can't understand.

Cutler nods, indicating down the hedgerow. Whitehead turns his head.

CUT TO:

JACOB, covered in blood and shit, stumbles out of the hedgerow and trips over Friend's body, slumping heavily to the ground.

(JACOB: A soldier. A veteran of European campaigns.)

CUT TO:

Whitehead staggers down the hedgerow towards Jacob and Friend in shock.

CUT TO:

Cutler looks back from Whitehead to Trower.

Cutler releases the pike from Trower's chest.

Cutler steals the shoes from Trower's feet, and puts them on.

Cutler looks out into the field with a grim expression.

Cutler unceremoniously cuts the ring finger from Trower's dead hand.

Cutler throws the finger over his shoulder into the long grass with disinterest.

Cutler pockets the ring and sets off down the field, using the bloody broken pike as a staff.

CUT TO:

Whitehead joins Jacob, who is stooped over Friend.

Whitehead's expression is one of concern, although his thoughts are mostly with himself.

Jacob's is irritated and tired.

Jacob does not look up during the following…

WHITEHEAD
Has he passed?

Jacob nods once in the affirmative.

JACOB
Shame. Bit soft in the head but good with a pike.

WHITEHEAD
We should pray.

JACOB
Got anything to eat?

Whitehead shakes his head no.

WHITEHEAD
No, sir.

JACOB
Last thing I ate was a stoat. A Welsh one at that.

Jacob spits in disgust and sighs profoundly.

The men hear a particularly blood-curdling scream emanate from the other side of the hedge.

JACOB
Fuck it. I'm not going back over. What about you?

Whitehead looks over at Cutler, who approaches.

WHITEHEAD
My man is dead.

JACOB
I'm my own man.

WHITEHEAD
(WORRIED.)
There is another, my Master.

JACOB
There are always others. No doubt he will find you. They usually do. Especially if they want their boots cleaned or the boils on their arses burst. This war's not been run to my liking. Too much fucking marching about. Not enough grub. I'd give anything for a good stew and a belly full of beer.

Cutler joins Jacob and Whitehead.

CUTLER
I was stopped a ways into the field when I hear the commotion.

Jacob looks up at Whitehead for the first time.

Jacob expression changes quickly from weary to one of aggression.

JACOB
Argggghhhh!

Jacob attacks Whitehead, roaring at him like a bull.

Jacob is the stronger man.

Cutler drops the pike and tries to pull Jacob from Whitehead.

The following is delivered during the protracted tug…

CUTLER
Easy, friend.

CUTLER
He was with the other lot!

WHITEHEAD
I am not your enemy, sir!

CUTLER
Easy, now.

WHITEHEAD
I am no soldier!

Cutler pulls Jacob from Whitehead.

Cutler still holds Whitehead at arms' length, shaking him vigorously.

Jacob grabs at Whitehead and shakes him harder.

JACOB
What the fuck *are* you, then?

Whitehead tries to pull himself away.

WHITEHEAD
(MISERABLE.)
I am a coward, sir!

Jacob tugs himself from Cutler's grasp and turns on him with confusion and rage.

WHITEHEAD (CONT'D)
(FLUSTERED/ ENRAGED.)
And what of you? What dispensation do you claim? Who's side are you on?

CUTLER
There are no sides here, friend. Not this side of the hedgerow.

Jacob struggles enraged against Cutler's constraint.

Cutler's had enough. He grasps Jacob firmly.

CUTLER
Tell you what, friend. Stop fucking about and we might forge an alliance at the Ale House I passed earlier, what say you?

Jacob stops struggling and becomes gravely intent on Cutler.

Friend suddenly inhales with a loud snore and wakes.

Jacob, Cutler and Whitehead turn to look at Friend.

FRIEND
(BLEARY EYED.)
Did someone mention ale?

Cutler, Jacob and Whitehead look at Friend with disbelief.

CUT TO:

EXT. BLACK - DAY.

Black.

Drumming (see 'The Preparative' from The Six Calls to War)

CUT TO

EXT. FIELD - DAY.

Cutler, Jacob, Friend and Whitehead stumble through the grass.

The hedgerow is directly behind them. The sound of battle dims.

Cutler leads the men, using the bloodied broken pike as a walking stick or staff.

Whitehead looks conflicted.

WHITEHEAD
I should go back and suffer the consequence of my failed mission.

JACOB
What mission would that be, Mary? Pegging out the wash?

WHITEHEAD
I am not at liberty to discuss my Master's business.

FRIEND
(TO CUTLER/INNOCENT.)
Perhaps he's right. Perhaps we should *all* go back and suffer. I feel that is what I do best anyway.

WHITEHEAD
Jesus Christ could be here any minute. We wouldn't want him to find us running away.

Jacob grabs Whitehead violently by the scruff of the neck.

Jacob throws Whitehead back, dangling him, and holds a clenched fist to his squashed cheek.

JACOB
(RAGING.)
We're not running away, we're going for a beer. Right?

Friend's face is upside down in the following Whitehead POV.

FRIEND
(TO WHITEHEAD.)
Perhaps he is right. Beer has it's own way of sorting things out, does it not?

CUT TO:

CUTLER
Forwards is back, 'tis all the same. God will find all as easy over a card table as swinging from tree.

Cutler looks with meaning at Whitehead.

Jacob lets go of Whitehead, who drops to the floor.

CUT TO:

Friend helps Whitehead up.

WHITEHEAD
Many thanks.

Friend sees that he has made Whitehead's hand muddy with his own filthy hand.

FRIEND
Sorry.

CUT TO:

Feeling embarrassed, he spits in Whitehead's hand and rubs it vigorously to remove the dirt with his own filthy shirt front.

Whitehead looks disgusted as he hobbles on.

CUT TO:

JACOB
(TO CUTLER.)
Got orders to catch this fella once. Stole a tablecloth. There was no tree to hang him from though, see. We'd burnt 'em all for firewood. Difficult business hanging a man without a tree.

CUT TO:

Whitehead is almost physically pained by talk and worry.

FRIEND
You alright?

WHITEHEAD
I am not a soldier. I am not accustomed to this- this- trajectory.

JACOB
Go back, then!

Cutler becomes irritated with Jacob's meddling.

CUTLER
(TO JACOB.)
He must not go back.

(TO WHITEHEAD.)
Your man said you would hang, did he not? Can you be certain all *his* loyal men are dead and do not wait to wring your neck like a wet mop?

You are as good as dead to them this side of the hedgerow. Leave it at that, surely friend.

Whitehead looks fearful, conflicted, thoughtful as he walks on.

WHITEHEAD
Well if God Almighty shall preserve my life, I may hereafter add many things and much light unto my art.

FRIEND
(TO JACOB.)
What's he say?

JACOB
He says, next time his master sends him on a job, he won't fuck it up.

FRIEND nods, satisfied.

JACOB
(TO CUTLER.)
Say, I see nothing but shit and thistles all about. Where is this ale house, exactly?

CUTLER
(TO JACOB.)
Across the field and beyond.

JACOB
(TO CUTLER.)
And you are paying, you say?

Cutler nods and looks at Whitehead

CUTLER
(TO WHITEHEAD.)
You'll eat first, though.

(TO JACOB.)
I have fire, a pot and something in it that I was working at when I heard that business in the lane. If nothing else it'll line your stomachs.

CUT TO:

Whitehead is gripped by indecision.

FRIEND
(TO WHITEHEAD. SOFT.)
You'll not go back?

WHITEHEAD
I am not accustomed to making decisions, yet self-preservation fuels me I admit.

FRIEND
We shall sample a better quality of suffering in this man's company, I feel certain.

Whitehead, grim-faced, walks on encouraged by Friend.

CUT TO:

Jacob looks over his shoulder before conferring with Cutler.

JACOB
(CONFIDENTIAL.)
We shall stop for but a short time though? I may not be running, but I have no desire to linger in these parts. I am only too aware that the odds are presently against a man living his full span.

Cutler stops abruptly.

CUTLER
(TO ALL.)
Listen.

Everyone stops and listens.

We hear Jacob's grumbling stomach.

The sound of the battle is fading.

CUTLER
They have already forgotten you.

WHITEHEAD
I wish the feeling were mutual.

CUTLER
The skirmish is moving elsewhere.

The men look about themselves at the stillness and beauty of the field for a long time, and at each other.

Jacob looks momentarily sanguine.

JACOB
Fuck 'em then for being so flighty.

WHITEHEAD
But surely someone will come after us?

Cutler puts his arm around Whitehead's shoulder with a patriarchal air.

CUTLER
Only shadows here, remember?

Friend watches Cutler and Whitehead walk off.

FRIEND
True to say, it would not be the first time *I* have left a wake of indifference behind me.

Cutler continues walking with Whitehead, using the pike as a walking stick.

Whitehead looks pained but somehow relieved by Cutler's embrace.

Cutler lets go of Whitehead.

Friend jogs up besides Whitehead.

FRIEND (CONT'D)
(TO WHITEHEAD.)
I was a cooper at Wickford in Essex before I joined.

WHITEHEAD
(DISTRACTED.)
Oh?

FRIEND
Have you been at Wickford?

WHITEHEAD
No. I never have.

FRIEND
Course you haven't. Quite right too.

Friend prods Whitehead in the chest.

FRIEND (CONT'D)
…You're a wise sort. I could tell from your

hands. Clean and soft. You think about a thing before you touch it, am I right?

WHITEHEAD
Is that not usual?

FRIEND
Not in Essex.

Whitehead raises an eyebrow.

FRIEND
Recruiters came to our village and sang a song about the glories of the battle. Course it isn't anything like that when your hands are in the business of fighting. But I still have the song.

Friend taps his head with his finger.

FRIEND (CONT'D)
...What about you?

WHITEHEAD
(WITH GROWING MISERY.)

An assistant to a gentleman at Norwich. An eminent Alchemist, physician and Astrologer amongst other things. I was charged with the compilation of sundry details for his almanacs and charts to aid his prominent friends, patrons and politicians in their decisions. All of great rank and fortune. I was often given leave of his library, which holds many closely guarded tombs, to educate myself. My Father's poverty forced me to leave school early but the Master saw something of a student in me.

Whitehead is miserable.

FRIEND
(CONFUSED.)
Astrologer you say?

WHITEHEAD
Yes. The celestial bodies. Their movements?

Whitehead points a finger up at he sky and twirls it.

WHITEHEAD (CONT'D)
...Prediction. Prophecy. Divination.

Friend looks confused.

WHITEHEAD (CONT'D)
...They hang above us. The stars? The planets?

FRIEND
No.

WHITEHEAD
Have you never looked up?

Friend is unimpressed. He shakes his head no.

FRIEND
(TO WHITEHEAD.)
Sounds badly paid.

WHITEHEAD
My Master says knowledge is its own payment.

Friend looks unconvinced.

FRIEND
(UNCONVINCED.)
The only knowledge I have is that God controls my fate as he pleases. I try to draw consolation from that.

Friend winces in pain.

FRIEND (CONT'D)
...Though I would like to know which of my many faults he is punishing me for at present.

Friend looks unconvinced by his own words.

WHITEHEAD
My Master says that whilst we live in fear of hell, we have it.

Friend pulls away from Whitehead, and looks at him with suspicion as they walk.

Cutler gives Whitehead a guarded backward glance.

CUT TO:

JACOB
(TO CUTLER.)
What line of business are you in, sir? You strike me as a man of the world.

CUTLER
Urghh.

Grasping at something.

CUTLER (CONT'D)
… Buttons.

Jacob raises an eyebrow in genuine surprise.

He winces and grasps his balls.

CUT TO:

Whitehead looks back at the hedge, over his shoulder.

FRIEND V.O
(SINGING.)
Baloo, my boy, lie still and sleep.

It grieves me sore to hear thee weep.

CUT TO:

The body of Trower, slowly engulfed by smoke drifting over from the battlefield.

FRIEND V.O (CONT'D)
…If thou'lt be silent, I'll be glad

Thy moaning makes my heart full sad.

EXT. FIELD - MUSHROOM RING - DAY.

Cutler picks MUSHROOMS and fills a HESSIAN SACK.

FRIEND V.O (CONT'D)
(SINGING.)
Baloo, my boy, thy mother's joy

Thy father bred me great annoy

Baloo, baloo, baloo, baloo

Baloo, baloo, lu-li-li-lu.

EXT. FIELD - COOKING POT - DAY.

Whitehead watches Friend stoke the small fire with twigs under the cooking pot in which a thin gruel bubbles.

FRIEND (CONT'D)
(SINGING.)
O'er thee I keep my lonely watch

Intent thy lightest breath to catch

O, when thou wak'st to see thee smile

And thus my sorrow to beguile.

Baloo, my boy, thy mother's joy

EXT. FIELD - A BUSH - DAY.

Jacob is constipated. He squats, breaches around his ankles, balls skirting nettles, labouring to squeeze out a shit.

FRIEND V.O (CONT'D)
(SINGING.)
Thy father bred me great annoy

Baloo, my boy, lie still and sleep

It grieves me sore to hear thee weep…

EXT. FIELD - MUSHROOM RING - DAY.

Cutler picks the last mushroom he needs, stands and throws the sack over his shoulder.

FRIEND V.O (CONT'D)
(SINGING.)
Twelve weary months have crept away

Since he, upon thy natal day

Left thee and me, to seek afar

A bloody fate in doubtful war.

JACOB V.O
(STRAINING HARDER.)
Argghhhhh.

EXT. FIELD - COOKING POT - DAY.

FRIEND
(SINGING.)
Baloo, my boy, lie still and sleep

It grieves me sore to hear thee weep

If thou'lt be silent, I'll be glad

Thy moaning makes my heart full sad….

Friend stops singing, sniffs the concoction.

WHITEHEAD
Mutton?

JACOB V.O
(STRAINING.)
Argghhhhh.

Friend looks around the field.

FRIEND
Where?

EXT. FIELD - A BUSH - DAY.

Whitehead and Friend round the bush and look upon Jacob straining miserably.

FRIEND
(TO JACOB.)
Boy or girl?

Jacob roars at Friend and falls into the bed of nettles, shrieking as his balls and arse are pricked.

FRIEND V.O
(SINGING.)
I dreamed a dream but yesternight

Thy father slain in foreign fight

EXT. FIELD - COOKING POT - DAY.

Cutler dumps mushrooms and herbs into the stew unseen by the others and stirs it meditatively.

FRIEND V.O (CONT'D)
(SINGING.)
He, wounded, stood beside my bed

His blood ran down upon thy head

EXT. FIELD - A BUSH - DAY.

Friend and Whitehead help Jacob up from the nettle bed.

FRIEND V.O (CONT'D)
(SINGING.)
He spoke no word, but looked on me

Bent low, and gave a kiss to thee!

Baloo, baloo, my darling boy

Thou'rt now alone thy mother's joy.

CUT TO:

Fire and the cooking pot.

CUT TO:

EXT. FIELD - COOKING POT - DAY.

Jacob is laid on his back in misery, his legs open to air his balls.

CUTLER
A merry band, are we not?

Cutler hands Whitehead a bowl of stew, numerous mushrooms bob on its greasy surface.

WHITEHEAD
Formed merely by the alchemy of circumstance. We would not otherwise associate.

Jacob raises an eyebrow.

JACOB
(TO WHITEHEAD.)
Many chums have you, back home?

Whitehead looks affronted and superior.

FRIEND
(TO JACOB.)
He has mostly been amongst books.

Whitehead puts down his bowl.

JACOB
My balls scream like harpies.

Cutler pauses as he fills a second bowl, then continues.

CUTLER
Nevertheless, 'tis indeed a pleasure to find like-minded company in such remote parts.

FRIEND
(TO WHITEHEAD.)
Where am I?

WHITEHEAD
(TO FRIEND.)
Monmouthshire.

Friend thinks hard.

FRIEND
Near Essex, is it?

WHITEHEAD
No.

JACOB
(TO WHITEHEAD.)
Don't bother.

Jacob taps the side of his head.

JACOB
…He hears the call and puts one foot in front of the other, is that not so, brother?

Friend nods in agreement.

FRIEND
(TO JACOB.)
I wonder where the others are now?

JACOB
North.

WHITEHEAD
My Master predicts that impending events will stagger the Monarch and Kingdom.

JACOB
From the Ale House, I stagger southeast.

WHITEHEAD
I believe I have distant relatives at Gloucester. I might go there.

FRIEND
Perhaps they have a large linen cupboard in which you can hide.

Whitehead looks miserable.

Jacob snatches the bowl from Cutler gruffly and sniffs it.

JACOB
(GUARDED.)
No stoat in this, is there?

Cutler shakes his head.

CUTLER
None.

Jacob, satisfied, begins eating without ceremony.

Whitehead looks at Jacob with disgust and puts his hands together in pray.

WHITEHEAD
We give thee humble thanks for this thy special bounty; beseeching thee to continue

thy loving kindness unto us, that our land may yield us her fruits of increase, to thy glory and our comfort: through Jesus Christ our Lord. Amen.

Friend starts eats with gusto.

Whitehead still does not eat.

CUTLER
Long walk that, Gloucester.

WHITEHEAD
If you follow the lanes.

CUTLER
Better done on a full stomach.

Whitehead thinks.

JACOB
(TO CUTLER.)
Sell a lot of them, do you?

CUTLER
(CONFUSED.)
What?

JACOB
Buttons.

CUTLER
(Sinister.)
Yeah, loads.

FRIEND
Rabbit?

Cutler shakes his head.

CUTLER
No.

Friend fishes out a chunk of bone from his mouth.

FRIEND
Which end of the mysterious beast do I have, then?

CUTLER
(IRRITATED.)
The arse end.

Jacob smiles with pleasure at this comment and makes a fucking gesture with his fingers.

Friend looks miserable as he drops the bone into the bowl.

Cutler looks at Whitehead, who still does not eat.

CUTLER (CONT'D)
There is nothing like a gnawing hunger to slow a man's pace. Eat.

Whitehead closely examining a cross-section of mushroom.

WHITEHEAD
Or fix a man's resolve.

Cutler becomes irritated by Whitehead's close observation of the mushroom.

CUTLER
Eat it, man. You don't have to marry it.

Whitehead does not eat and sets the mushroom carefully back into the bowl in front of him.

WHITEHEAD
I cannot. I am set on a particular fast.

Jacob slurps the last of his stew from his bowl.

JACOB
Give it here then, Mary.

Jacob grabs Whitehead's bowl and eats that too.

Belches loudly.

JACOB (CONT'D)
Bit sour, but passable.

CUT TO:

Whitehead takes a crumpled astrological chart from his pocket and examines it with grave intensity.

CUT TO:

Jacob throws the empty bowl aside and lays back satisfied.

JACOB (CONT'D)

No more orders. No more marching. What about women at this ale house?

Cutler nods yes.

CUTLER

There is plenty of distraction to be had in these parts.

Jacob smiles with satisfaction, then catches Whitehead's disapproving eye.

JACOB
What? A pair of English tits not good enough for you?

Cutler smiles coldly.
Cutler lights Friend's clay pipe and considers Whitehead with great irritation.

Friend thinks, then pats his pockets.

FRIEND
'Tis indeed a blessed relief to be forgotten.

Cutler nods and smokes with pleasure, puffing away extravagantly, his face is increasingly obscured by a cloud of smoke.

CULTER V.O
If I might ask a favour of you boys now that you have shared my food.

CUT TO:

EXT. FIELD - DAY.

A drifting smoke fills the field like a greater, dreamlike version of Cutler's smoking.

EXT. FIELD - A WOODEN STAKE - DAY.

Tableau vivant: Cutler addresses the troops. Cutler, Jacob, Friend and Whitehead are gathered around a LARGE WOODEN STAKE driven firmly into the earth. Wound and knotted around the stake is a sturdy ROPE, which leads off into the long grass out of shot.

Under this, drumming (see 'The Troop' from The Six Calls to War).

Jacob rubs his eyes and head, groggily.

JACOB
(PISSED OFF.)
Sounds more like an order.

Whitehead crouches down, looks at the wooden stake with a furrowed brow.
Cutler meets Whitehead's eye.

CUTLER
I won't stand by like some gentleman while you pull more than your fair share.

Cutler meets Jacob's eye.

CUTLER
I shall take my weight right along with you.

CUT TO:

Friend crouches down next to Whitehead and examines the wooden stake, which on closer inspection is intricately carved with a ring of dancing figures around its head.

FRIEND
(THOUGHTFUL.)
Rowan wood.

CUT TO:

Whitehead stands.

WHITEHEAD
(TO CUTLER.)
What's at the end?

Jacob waves a dismissive, silencing hand at Whitehead.

JACOB
Hang on. Hang on. More important what of the alehouse?

Cutler ignores Whitehead.

CUTLER
(TO JACOB.)
After.

Friend stands with difficulty, as if woozy.

FRIEND
(TO CUTLER.)
You know, that's a fine stake you've got there. I'll give you that.

JACOB
I don't pull well on an empty pocket.

Whitehead wanders off a way, to look across the field.

Cutler follows him with his eyes.

CUTLER
Every man has his price.

Cutler digs in his pocket.

JACOB
My price is not buttons. The country has had all my charity.

Cutler throws down a collection of gold rings at Jacob's feet.

Jacob is genuinely surprised.

CUTLER
(DISMISSIVE.)
Take your pick.

Cutler walks after Whitehead.

CUT TO:

Jacob crouches to examine the rings and misshapen lumps of gold, which transfix him.

JACOB
I'll be jiggered.

We see Jacob's saucer eyes, fixed.
We see the rings in detail. Some caked in blood, other's in mud.

Jacob chooses the ring from Trower's finger. (Distinctive because of its design.)

CUT TO:

Friend, who has gone back to fondling the wooden stake with pleasure like a large dildo, looks dreamy; spaced out…

FRIEND
(APPRECIATIVELY.)
Someone knows his wood.

CUT TO:

Whitehead nudges the rope with the toe of his threadbare shoe.

Cutler quietly joins Whitehead.

CUTLER
You won't eat.

Whitehead is startled from his thoughts.

WHITEHEAD
I do not suffer the same hunger as our friends.

Cutler watches Whitehead's toe nudge the rope.

WHITEHEAD(CONT'D)
I believe they would sell any religion for a jug of beer.

Whitehead looks back at Cutler, who is smiling thinly.

Whitehead notices for the fist time a gold coin tied around Cutler's neck (the gold 'Angel' distributed by Charles I to those suffering scrofula).

WHITEHEAD (CONT'D)
You have an angel about you.

Cutler looks unnerved for the first time.

Whitehead reaches for the necklace.

WHITEHEAD (CONT'D)
You were touched for the King's evil.

What was it like to look upon his Majesty?

Cutler looks surprised.

CUTLER
Curiosity fuels you then, not food. Let the king worry on his own magic. God knows he needs it. I, however, need yours.

Whitehead pulls further and reveals a fist full of gold amulets dangling there.

Cutler smiles menacingly and draws back a little.

Whitehead's brow furrows on seeing this unusual collection.

Cutler grabs his hand.

Cutler stamps his foot down on top of Whitehead's foot, which has all along been nudging the rope, and grinds it with the heel of his boot.

Whitehead winces as his eye falls to Cutler's hand on his pistol.

CUTLER (CONT'D)
Pull, coward.

Black.

EXT. FIELD - A ROPE - DAY.

Under this, drumming (see 'The March' from The Six Calls to War)

Jacob roars with exertion as he pulls on the rope.

CUT TO:

Cutler gathers some belongings, including the pike end and a clean WHITE SHIRT. He puts the shirt in the hessian sack and throws it over his shoulder.

CUT TO:

Jacob & Friend pulling hard on the rope.

Whitehead watches, in a reticent, assessing fashion, from the side lines.

CUT TO:

Cutler catches Whitehead's eye with a threatening look as he bears his teeth and shows the butt of his gun.

CUT TO:

Whitehead sees that with just two men pulling, with all their strength, no progress is made.

Whitehead looks out into the grass, along the taut rope, at nothing.

Whitehead makes a reluctant decision.

Whitehead steps towards the rope. Cutler sees him and smiles.

Whitehead steps into line behind Friend and begins to pull.
Cutler falls in behind Whitehead and sets to the pull as well.

Under this, drumming (see 'The March' from The Six Calls to War)

The rope shifts infinitesimally but instantly.

The first coil of rope drops by the rowan stake.

They appear to pull back at an acute angle but are in fact pulled forward through the grass.

The boys' feet slip forward a few inches to the edge of a MUSHROOM CIRCLE.

CUTLER
Hold fast!

With each pull they are dragged forward, not back, as if they are losing at a tug of war.

JACOB
(IMPOTENT RAGE.)
Argggggghh!

They are oblivious to their loss of ground.

They enter the magical realm by degrees.

The job takes considerable time and effort. They all sweat profusely.

Cutler pulls on the rope with cold determination.

CUT TO:

Jacob pulls on the rope with curses and boiling rage.

CUT TO:

Friend pulls on the rope as he hums his recruiting song under his breath.

CUT TO:

Whitehead pulls on the rope, eyes closed, teeth gritted.

CUT TO:

The field in smoke.

The sounds of the men straining against the rope

are still running under this, along with distant voices…

TROWER V.O
You shall hang from the nearest tree.

FRIEND V.O
Which end of the beast do I have?

CUT TO:

Whitehead's straining face, eyes closed.

CUTLER V.O
What do you see, friend?

WHITEHEAD V.O
Shadows.

CUT TO:

We are now within the mushroom ring.

CUTLER
He's coming!

CUT TO:

Whitehead opens his eyes.

Jacob looks disgusted, confused, but does not stop pulling.

JACOB
A man?

CUTLER
Pull!

CUT TO:

We see a bruised, battered and muddy man, O'NEIL, laid out in the long grass with the straining rope tied about his person. Eyes open wide, unblinking, as if frozen.

JACOB V.O
Is that's all?

FRIEND V.O
A cripple perhaps?

(O'NEIL: A man. Bare chested, ragged trousers, bruised and covered in burns.)

CUT TO:

The boys are dragged along inch by inch towards O'Neil.

CUTLER
Pull!

(The normal effort required to pull one man is far less than that which is being utilized, suggesting an unnatural occurrence is underway.)

FRIEND
Maybe he is uncommonly fat? I once had to pull my father-in-law from a bog.

Whitehead strains and looks concerned.

JACOB
You are in possession of a wife! I would not have thought it possible.

FRIEND
Perhaps still. There was a misunderstanding before I left home concerning a small fire.

Friend's eyes wonder across the sky, distracted from the work at hand and the conversation.

FRIEND
What beautiful colours.

Cutler spies the first glimpses of O'Neil through the grass.

CUTLER
He's coming!

JACOB
(TO O'NEIL.)
Get up you lazy bastard!

FRIEND
Why does he not get up!

CUTLER
Pull damn you!

WHITEHEAD
(ADAMANT.)
No… more… pulling!

Whitehead suddenly lets go of the rope.

CUT TO:

Friend, Jacob and Cutler tumble forward like dominos.

(Perhaps a flurry of drumming here and then it comes to a full stop.)

Friend falls heavily on Cutler.

Black.

CUTLER V.O
Sir?

CUT TO:

The screen is full of O'Neil's eye. the pupil is black.

CUTLER V.O
Sir?

CUT TO:

EXT. FIELD - INSIDE THE CIRCLE - DAY.

Cutler stoops over O'Neil, their faces close. Cutler looking intently into O'Neil's face.

CUTLER
I have brought assistance.

O'Neil closes his eyes.

CUT TO:

O'Neil is beating Cutler mercilessly.

Cutler does not defend himself. He is on the floor in a crumpled heap.

CUTLER
I am not your enemy, sir!

CUT TO:

Jacob and Friend stand mesmerized as they watch Cutler get the shit kicked out of him.

JACOB
We should intervene.

Whitehead looks grim-faced and crosses his arms.

WHITEHEAD
That is he.

JACOB
Who?

WHITEHEAD
O'Neil. The man I was charged with locating. Then I am vindicated.

Jacob shakes his head, as if clearing his thoughts and attends to the situation at hand.

JACOB
Right.

CUT TO:

Jacob labours to pull O'Neil from Cutler.

JACOB
Easy now.

But O'Neil continues to fight the air as Cutler staggers out of his master's reach.

CUTLER
I am not your enemy!

Friend and Whitehead come to Jacob's assistance, to restrain the violently thrashing man.

JACOB
(BUSINESSLIKE.)
Hold him tight, boys.

When Whitehead and Friend have as firm a grip on O'Neil as can be expected, Jacob comes around in front.

JACOB
(TO O'NEIL.)
Beg pardon.

Jacob punches O'Neil hard in the face.

Black.

(Under this some kind of sounds/music/noise-scape like something suffering/trapped/ethereal.)

O'NEIL V.O
(HURRIED.)
Erect your Figure aright, consider the several aspects of the Planets, if there be in the ascendant, or in any Angle a Fortune, say, there is Treasure in the ground, and that the thing hid is still in the ground, the quality, price, esteem thereof shall be according to the potency, virtue or debility of the Fortune.

EXT. FIELD - TREE STUMP - DAY.

Music.

O'Neil is now conscious and composed and sits stiff-backed on a log as Cutler undoes the rope and drops it on the ground.

O'NEIL
Apologies, Cutler. I was entranced.

Cutler winces as he attends O'Neil, struggling to mask the pain of his beating.

CUTLER
That's quite alright, sir.

CUT TO:

Jacob, Whitehead and Friend sit at some distance.

Jacob and Friend show signs of their debilitation.

CUT TO:

Cutler attends O'Neil reverently on bent knee.

He gives O'Neil his guns.

CUTLER
(TO O'NEIL.)
Sorry I was so long. There was a skirmish in the lane. Worked in my favour though. Thinned out our pursuers.

CUT TO:

Whitehead eyes O'Neil with determined distraction.

WHITEHEAD
You men will assist me in his detainment.

CUT TO:

Jacob, preoccupied, grabs at his crotch, looks concerned, fumbles around.

JACOB
Hello?

CUT TO:

Friend is watching his hand, dance through the air and in front of Whitehead's face.

FRIEND
Like gossamer.

Whitehead swats it away like a fly.

WHITEHEAD
(TO FRIEND, IRRITATED.)
What is it with you and hands?

CUT TO:

Cutler buttons the crisp white shirt, taken from his bag, across O'Neil's wounded torso.

CUTLER
(TO O'NEIL.)
Kings men are disillusioned. All endure privations. News is that Cromwell's men are marching north to meet the Engagers. I heard he exacted terrible revenge on the Welsh bastards at Pembroke, sir…

O'NEIL
(GRUMPY.)
Indeed.

O'Neil puts out his hand.

O'NEIL (CONT'D)
…This Irish bastard requires his mirror.

CUTLER
Sorry, sir.

Cutler produces a POLISHED BLACK DISC from the bag, which he places in O'Neil hand.

O'NEIL
You will have ample time to indulge your politics when we have parted company, Cutler.

CUTLER
Yes, sir.

O'NEIL
There is nothing beyond this field that concerns you at present.

CUT TO:

Jacob looks over at the BLACK DISC.

JACOB
What's that he holds?

Whitehead's expression turns grave as he watches O'Neil with the mirror.

WHITEHEAD
(CONCERNED/SPECULATING.)
A scrying mirror.

Jacob speaks to his crotch, distracted, as he fumbles with himself…

JACOB
A whatings what?

WHITEHEAD
An occult tool. A means for telling the past, present, perhaps even future. The visions therein can come from God, spirits, the Devil even, if the user is gifted. He must have utilized some diabolical method to conceal his presence in the field. That is why he was not visible.

CUT TO:

Cutler produces a comb from the bag and combs O'Neil's greasy hair straight back.

O'Neil considers his own distorted reflection in the disc with critical satisfaction.

JACOB V.O
You think he sees what an arse he looks sat there like the king himself?

WHITEHEAD
No.

CUT TO:

O'Neil catches Whitehead's reflection in the mirror.

CUT TO:

Cutler looks over at the Whitehead.

Jacob has dropped down on his knees beside him.

CUTLER
Wasn't sure which one he was at first. A cowardly type though. You should not have any trouble with him.

CUT TO:

Whitehead looks at Friend, who is transfixed by his own hand, which is firmly planted over his own face.

CUTLER V.O (CONT'D)
He's the one did not eat the mushrooms.

O'NEIL
I know which he is, Cutler. What I do not know is why he comes equipped with bridesmaids.

CUT TO:

Whitehead looks at Jacob, who is down on his hands and knees searching about in the grass, one hand grasping his balls.

CUT TO:

Cutler helping O'Neil up.

CUTLER
The other two are cattle to help with the pull and the dig. The quicker we are done sir, the quicker we can leave, is it not?

CUT TO:

Whitehead stoops over Jacob, addressing him with irritation and mounting stress.

WHITEHEAD
What are you doing? Get up!

JACOB
I don not feel 'em.

WHITEHEAD
What?

JACOB
My balls. They've ceased screaming.

WHITEHEAD
That is good, is it not? It means the nettle's sting has run its course.

JACOB
They always scream. It is unnatural for them not to.

Jacob squeezes his crotch.

JACOB (CONT'D)
…Maybe I mislaid them while putting the rope.

CUT TO:

O'Neil passes the scrying mirror back to Cutler.

O'NEIL
He refused to eat, you say?

CUTLER
Yes, sir.

O'NEIL
He has no manners.

CUT TO:

Whitehead crosses his arms defiantly as O'Neil approaches.

O'NEIL V.O (CONT'D)
Let us hope there are no other holes in his education.

CUT TO:

Cutler bugs O'Neil as they walk.

CUTLER
(WORRIED.)
You have the means to escape the field, sir? Hidden within your books and wotnots? The magic is strong. The pull was hard. To tell the truth, the thought of spending my share of the treasure is all that gives courage.

O'Neil is irritated by Cutler's practical inquiry.

O'NEIL
Don't think, Cutler… dig.

CUT TO:

O'Neil puts his hand out to shake with Whitehead.

O'NEIL (CONT'D)
Whitehead.

WHITEHEAD
O'Neil.

Whitehead looks at O'Neil's outstretched hand, which has drawn all over it cryptic markings.

WHITEHEAD
I have my quarry, sir.

O'NEIL
You were expected, sir.

Whitehead does not unfold his arms, but looks surprised and confused by O'Neil's greeting.

WHITEHEAD
Indeed?

O'Neil smiles grimly and drops his hand unshaken.

O'NEIL
It has been some time since we shared company. Things have changed.

WHITEHEAD
(SPEACHIFYING.)
Not so the law. In the absence of better qualified men, sir, I hereby place you under arrest for the theft of certain documents from the private collection of my Master. In the presence of our Merciful God, I trust you will now surrender yourself and return willingly to Norwich, to face your accuser.

O'NEIL
And how is our Master?

Whitehead is alarmed, confused by O'Neil's lack of compliance.

WHITEHEAD
Well, I pray.

O'Neil puts his arm around Whitehead and leads him off.

O'NEIL
I bet he still makes you do a lot of that. Pray, I mean.

Whitehead looks back towards Jacob and Friend.

WHITEHEAD
The Master is of advanced years as you know. You're outrageous pillage has greatly aggravated his dropsy.

O'NEIL
No doubt he would have come himself. Instead he sends you, the faithful servant.

CUT TO:

Friend holds a shovel, with the face of it close to his face, obscuring his features.

CUT TO:

Jacob is looking down the front of his own trousers when Cutler shoves an identical shovel at him.

JACOB
(DISTRACTED.)
What the fuck is this?

Friend speaks from behind the shovel head…

FRIEND
It is a shovel.

JACOB
(RAGING.)
I know what it is!

Cutler nudges Jacob with the barrel of a gun.

CUTLER
Move.

Cutler shoves Friend hard with the gun.

FRIEND
What kind of 'merry band' is this?!

CUT TO:

O'Neil puts his arm around Whitehead's shoulder and steers him away into the field, with the self-assured air of a lord of the ,anor.

O'NEIL
Come. Walk. You need no invitation. This is your country, is it not? Although I have claimed a small corner of it which I am in-

tent on raping it a little. 'Tis only fair that I take something in return for my countrymen's troubles.

CUT TO:

Cutler, Jacob and Friend move off, following O'Neil and Whitehead.

O'NEIL (CONT'D)
Cutler marked you as a coward. It is comforting to know things have not changed greatly in my absence.

Whitehead looks startled and ashamed.

WHITEHEAD
'Tis true that I hid in a bush as Mr. Trower and his men were set upon.

O'NEIL
Trower, the dunderhead mercenary.

Whitehead nods his head miserably.

O'NEIL (CONT'D)
How is he?

WHITEHEAD
Dead.

O'NEIL
Then your arrest is academic, would you say?

WHITEHEAD
Unless you comply freely, as a Christian man.

O'NEIL
The Master has kept you a veritable virgin as to the workings of the world.

WHITEHEAD
It is true I have been mostly amongst books.

Whitehead looks back at Jacob and Friend.

WHITEHEAD (CONT'D)
…I find pages easier to turn than people.

O'Neil pats Whitehead heavily on the shoulder.

WHITEHEAD (CONT'D)
I confess, I have acquired one new skill since your absence.

O'NEIL
Indeed?

WHITEHEAD
(COY.)
Lacemaking.

O'Neil raises an eyebrow.

WHITEHEAD (CONT'D)
(TRIPPING ON HIS WORDS.)
Only in my spare time, which is limited, because of my increased duties in your absence, but of the highest quality I am told.

O'Neil looks mystified by Whitehead's lack of self-knowledge.

O'NEIL
He has not only kept you a stranger to the world but to yourself.

WHITEHEAD
I do not follow.

O'NEIL
You will. Unfortunately my constitution was not suited to the Master's pious regiment. I am forced to branch out on my own. I owe money everywhere. To so many I lose track. Perhaps even to God.

Whitehead looks shocked and disgusted.

O'NEIL (CONT'D)
…We shall spend some time in continental Europe when the opportunity arises.

O'Neil is pleased with his effect.

O'NEIL (CONT'D)
…I have had little success up to now at applying the Master's arts, to finding anything of great worth, which is why I have conjured you.

Whitehead stops in astonishment.

O'Neil stops abruptly and indicates the field.

O'NEIL (CONT'D)
…This place holds a great treasure. I am certain of that. I merely require a finer eye to pin-point the particular location. As much as I detest you personally, Whitehead, I acknowledge that your gifts are stronger in certain areas.

WHITEHEAD
Thank you. But I must remind you that the practice of magic should be a holy quest. A search for knowledge by revelation.

O'NEIL
All well and good, but you are now my divining rod.

WHITEHEAD
I have little of my Master's art in divination. You are confused, sir. Tis I who am capturing you. Not the other way around.

O'Neil grasps Whitehead firmly and looks with deeply into Whitehead eyes.

O'NEIL
Do not concern yourself with heroics now, Whitehead. 'Tis official. You are now my prisoner.

Cutler throws another gun to O'Neil.

O'Neil points his own weapon at Whitehead's chest.

O'NEIL (CONT'D)
...You will find the treasure buried in this field.

O'Neil swings the barrel around to point at Cutler, Friend and Jacob...

O'NEIL (CONT'D)
...They will dig it up.

O'Neil points a ringed finger at himself.

O'NEIL (CONT'D)
...I will claim it.

Whitehead steels himself and is adamant.

WHITEHEAD
I will not assist you in such an ungodly scheme, sir.

O'Neil smiles menacingly and pats Whitehead heartily.

CUT TO:

Everyone walks in gloomy doom-laden silence.

Cutler keeps up the rear with his gun raised and ready.

O'Neil walks out in front in high spirits.

O'NEIL
(TO EVERYONE.)
The world is turned upside down Whitehead, and so is its pockets.

Whitehead turns from O'Neil, who is absorbed in his own smugness, to look around the field.

O'NEIL
(TO CUTLER/ PLEASED.)
Yes, make a note of that, Cutler, for my memoir and recollections.

Cutler rolls his eyes, unseen by O'Neil.

CUT TO:

Whitehead's eye falls on Jacob, who comes up beside him looking increasingly ill.

WHITEHEAD
(STAGGERED.)
I fear he has passed all bounds of Christianity.

JACOB
He dresses well, though.

Whitehead looks at Jacob with irritation, then notices Jacob's ill pallor.

WHITEHEAD
(TO JACOB.)
You are sick?

JACOB
(SNAPPING.)
No.
(BEFUDDLED/ RUBBING HIS BROW.)
Yes. My feet are lead. I feel like I walk yet make no progress. And there is a terrible burning like the fires of hell upon me.

WHITEHEAD
I have some knowledge of physic.

Whitehead looks around nervously, as they walk.

WHITEHEAD (CONT'D)
…I will attend you as soon as circumstance allows.

Jacob grabs his balls defensively.

JACOB
Fuck off.

Jacob is affronted, as if Whitehead has made a pass at him.

Whitehead pulls his chin in, his feelings hurt.

Jacob petitions O'Neil confidently...

JACOB (CONT'D)
(TO O'NEIL.)
Say, friend. My business with your man is concluded, if 'tis all the same I might bob off now. I confess I feel peaky. Could do with a few hours kip.

O'Neil hits Jacob across the face with the butt of his gun.

(Jacob is debilitated by his various ailments and impediments, so is running sluggish.)

Whitehead notes Cutler's gun trained on him.

CUT TO:

Friend presents Cutler with a large smile and an open expression, oblivious of Cutler's menace, as Jacob gets up from the floor.

FRIEND
(INDICATING O'NEIL.)
It does not surprise me that the Devil is an Irish man, but perhaps I thought a little taller?

Cutler looks at Friend like he's an idiot.

CUT TO:

O'Neil looks down on Jacob, with contempt.

O'NEIL
Do not address me as friend and do not speak to me directly again. Otherwise I shall turn you into a frog.

Jacob is miserable.

Whitehead helps Jacob up to his feet.

CUT TO:

CUTLER
(TO FRIEND.)
I am curious. Tell me. How did an idiot like you come to stay alive so long?

Friend thinks.

FRIEND
Commanding officer says I have fresh air between my ears. Fresh air is good for a man's constitution, is it not?

FRIEND
You may make a note of that.

Friend, satisfied with himself strides ahead, slinging his shovel over his shoulder.

Cutler sneers at Friend's impudence and shakes his head in dismay.

CUT TO:

Black.

Music.

CUT TO:

EXT. FIELD - CAMPSITE - DAY.

Music.

Drumming (see 'The March' from The Six Calls of War)

A modest TENT (perhaps surrounded by a circle of salt).

A smoldering campfire with a cook pot on top.

Magical books.

Other instruments and evidence of astrological and alchemical investigation.

A pile of filled earthenware wine bottles covered in a ragged square of waxed canvas.
Everything is in general disarray, giving the air of chaos and general sloppiness.

CUT TO:

Tableau vivant: O'Neil stands holding the door flap of the tent open. His other hand beckons Whitehead to enter. A little removed stands Cutler, with his gun pointed at Jacob and Friend, who kneel down with their hands in prayer, balanced on the butt of their shovel handles and their heads bent low.

(Under this, music continued from the previous.)

CUT TO:

Whitehead enters the tent followed by O'Neil.

The tent flap drops behind them (filling the whole screen).

There is a long time of suspense-filled silence when we only see the tent's canvas flap in close-up, accompanied by the sounds of the field, wind, birds, leaves until it is suddenly pierced by…

WHITEHEAD V.O
(SCREAMING IN AGONY.)
Arrggggghhhhh!

CUT TO:

Jacob lurches up from his kneeling position, towards the tent.

Cutler cracks Jacob with the butt of his gun.

JACOB
(RAGING IN FRUSTRATION.)
Argggghh!

Cutler smirks.

WHITEHEAD V.O
(SCREAMING IN AGONY.)
Arrggggghhhhh!

Whitehead is tortured mercilessly behind the tent's closed canvas flap.

CUT TO:

Friend plugs his ears with his fingers.

CUT TO:

Cutler moves a ragged wax canvas to reveal a pile of wine bottles.

CUTLER
(TO JACOB.)
Take courage.

Jacob's attention is completely distracted from the sounds of Whitehead's misery and his own bloodied head.

Cutler smirks again and throws Jacob a BOTTLE OF WINE.

CUT TO:

Friend chants loudly to mask the sound of Whitehead's misery.

Whitehead's misery is protracted.

FRIEND
(CHANTING.)
If wishes were horses

Beggars would ride:

If turnips were watches

I would wear one by my side.

If wishes were horses

…

CUT TO:

Jacob unplugs the wine bottle and drinks deeply.

FRIEND
(CHANTING.)
Beggars would ride:

If turnips were watches

I would wear one by my side.

If wishes were horses

Beggars would ride:

If turnips were watches

I would wear one by my side.

Wine streaming down Jacob's chin, staining his shirt.

CUT TO:

Jacob, Cutler and Friend turn as one to see Whitehead stumble out of the tent.

A rope is tied around Whitehead's neck. (Or some harness made of rope, with a wooden mouth-bit.)

CUT TO:

Jacob lets the bottle drop from his mouth in grim surprise.

JACOB
(BITTER.)
What this party lacks is the civilizing influence of women.

CUT TO:

Whitehead falls to the ground. He is seemingly unblemished, although unnaturally pale.

One drop of blood falls from his nose to the ground, the droplet is black.

Whitehead is a changed man. He has seen something dark and terrible.

CUT TO:

Cutler is somewhat dis-eased.

He battles to hide it behind a stoney expression of grim determination.

CUT TO:

Jacob takes a deep swig of wine and passes the bottle to Friend.

FRIEND
No thanks.

JACOB
Take it, you fool.

CUT TO:

Jacob and Whitehead make eye contact.

Whitehead challenges Jacob to intervene with his look.

CUT TO:

Friend takes a deep swig and gags, as if it is his first taste of wine.

Jacob grabs the bottle back.

JACOB
What vintage bile is this?

CUT TO:

O'Neil saunters out of the tent after a moment, with nonchalant satisfaction.

O'NEIL
Good. Now all know their place in this asterism.

Whitehead begins to weep with silent impotent rage into the dirt as O'Neil stoops down and pats Whitehead on the head like a dog.

O'NEIL
…To work.

CUT TO:

EXT. FIELD - DAY.

We are off a hunting…

The camera rushes through the grass.

We see the men's feet stomping.

EXT. FIELD - DAY.

Rousing music, as if for a hunt.

The boys make a large circumnavigation of the field at speed. They rush through the grass at a euphoric, frenetic pace, gripped by a hysteria as if on a dangerous fairground ride.

Whitehead strains at the rope tied around his neck.

FRIEND
(TO CUTLER.)
He seems like a nice enough fellow. Why do we race him like a nag to the glue pot?

Cutler ignores him.

Friend gallops ahead, and calls over his shoulder…

FRIEND (CONT'D)
No matter! I like it, whatever it is!

Friend waves his shovel in the air.

CUT TO:

O'Neil waves his gun in the air, perhaps firing it, causing a plume of smoke, and pulls hard to control Whitehead, who is fuelled by fear and magical madness.

O'NEIL
'Tis a golden breastplate you seek, Whitehead. The gems alone I believe worth some twenty-five thousand. If we find the Urim and Thummim, even more.

CUT TO:

Jacob swigs feverishly from the bottle as he stumbles.

CUT TO:

Friend snatches the bottle from Jacob.

CUT TO:

Cutler looks grim but determined.

CUT TO:

Clouds move above them as they spiral out of control, their motion increasing in speed and feverishness.

All is accompanied by a cacophony of discordant music rising to a climax.

CUT TO:

EXT. FIELD - CAMPSITE - DAY.

Whitehead suddenly drops to his knees, exhausted, on the same spot as where he started from outside the tent.

Music stops abruptly.

Whitehead's eyes fall on the droplet of blood which previously fell from his nose.

The droplet is black.

WHITEHEAD
Here.

CUT TO:

O'Neil, gasping for breath, smiles and pats Whitehead on the head.

O'NEIL
There.

CUT TO:

Friend takes a swig from the wine bottle. He is intoxicated by the wine and the events.

FRIEND
(TO O'NEIL/ EAGER.)
What would you have us do now, devil?

Jacob snatches the bottle back with contempt, shakes it, finds it empty.

Jacob throws the bottle into the grass.

JACOB
(TO FRIEND.)
Shut your buggering mouth.

CUT TO:

Cutler nudges Friend with his gun.

CUTLER
Dig.

CUT TO:

Jacob helps himself to another full wine bottle from the pile and pops the cork, catching Cutler's eye as he does.

O'NEIL
(TO WHITEHEAD.)
You must be thirsty.

Cutler snatches the bottle from Jacob and passes it to O'Neil.

CUT TO:

Jacob and Cutler are in silent agreement. They hate each other.

CUT TO:

O'Neil grabs the disorientated Whitehead in one hand and the bottle in the other.

CUT TO:

Friend breaks the earth with his shovel.

CUT TO:

O'Neil pulls Whitehead's head back at an acute angle.

O'NEIL (CONT'D)
Cutler tells me you declined his hospitality, but you *will* do me the honour, sir.

Whitehead struggles to release himself as O'Neil tries to force wine down his throat.

WHITEHEAD
You may break me, sir, but I will not break my oath.

O'Neil and Whitehead struggle, wine splashing on Whitehead's face.

O'NEIL
Open up now and let the devil in!

As the determined word escapes Whitehead's lips, O'Neil seizes the opportunity and pores wine down Whitehead's throat.

CUT TO:

Friend digs.

CUT TO:

Whitehead wretches, chokes.

CUT TO:

Jacob bears his red wine-stained teeth at Cut-ler.

CUT TO:

Whitehead throws up violently on the ground between himself and O'Neil.

CUT TO:

O'Neil steps back, revolted, and looks down at the contents of Whitehead's stomach.

CUT TO:

There in a puddle of undigested red wine lay 12 stones.

CUT TO:

O'Neil's expression changes from disgust to mild confusion.

He stoops to examine them at closer quarters.

Whitehead looks equally confused as O'Neil nudges the stones with a fingertip.

O'Neil looks up at Whitehead.

CUT TO:

Cutler nudges Jacob's attention from O'Neil and Whitehead with the barrel of his gun.

CUTLER
Get digging.

Jacob digs.

CUT TO:

O'Neil's self-assurance has slipped.

Whitehead is stunned and mystified.

WHITEHEAD
I have no recollection of consuming anything of the remotest sort.

O'Neil muses.

O'NEIL
A man can hold a great deal inside which he does not comprehend.

Beat.

O'NEIL (CONT'D)
…I am not familiar with these symbols.

WHITEHEAD
Nor I. I feel suddenly. Empty. Yet-

Whitehead would say 'changed', but does not, catching himself before he reveals himself.

O'NEIL
(FRUSTRATED.)
What?

Whitehead checks himself in the face of O'Neil's inquisition.

WHITEHEAD
(GUARDED/ CLAMMING UP.)
Nothing.

O'NEIL
You do best to keep your mouth closed then, in case something else should rush in while you are not paying attention. You are apparently nothing more than an envelope.

O'Neil rubs his head and waves his hand in Whitehead's face.

Whitehead takes some small pleasure from O'Neil's perplexity.

O'Neil's thoughts are fogged by madness.

O'NEIL (CONT'D)
I must consult my documents.

WHITEHEAD
(BOLD.)
The Master's, you mean.

O'Neil looks sharply at Whitehead.

Whitehead exhibits the whisperings of untapped impudence.

O'NEIL
Of course, you will have to be punished. Wait here. I will devise something.

Whitehead sags, losing confidence with the mention of torture.

O'Neil grabs up the stones from the ground.

Whitehead, suddenly suffocated by circumstance, grabs O'Neil's arm.

WHITEHEAD
I have located your treasure sir. Release me. Please.

Whitehead grimaces…

WHITEHEAD (CONT'D)
…I beg.

O'Neil smiles.

CUT TO:

Jacob stops digging, and observes Whitehead and O'Neil.

CUT TO:

O'NEIL
Don't be ridiculous, Whitehead. What you have given me is the place in which to make a hole. Nothing more. Perhaps you can fashion it a lace doily while we wait and see what is at the bottom of it.

Whitehead looks O'Neil in the eye, with cold hatred and abject self-loathing, having debased himself by begging.

He pushes past O'Neil, heading towards 'the hole'

CUT TO:

Jacob watches Whitehead approach.

CUT TO:

Cutler tracks Whitehead with raised gun.

Whitehead pick up a shovel and commences digging alongside Jacob and Friend.

Jacob stops and observes Whitehead with mild surprise.

WHITEHEAD
What?

Jacob smiles at Whitehead.

JACOB
Nothing, Mary. Only you seem to suffer more from things you think might happen than things that do.

WHITEHEAD
Great. Thanks. And what in God's name does that mean!

Jacob seems suddenly confused.

JACOB
(CONFUSED.)
I don't know. It just came out.

Jacob continues digging.

Friend stops digging.

FRIEND
(EXCITED.)
I think I have worked out what God is punishing us for.

Jacob and Whitehead turn to look at Friend.

FRIEND (CONT'D)
(TRIUMPHANT.)
Everything!

Jacob looks ill.

Jacob staggers.

Whitehead's expression turns from irritation to concern, as he grips Jacob's arm.

WHITEHEAD
O'Neil?

O'Neil turns as he about to enter his tent.

WHITEHEAD
This man is sick.

Jacob staggers, and sits heavily on his arse, grabbing his balls and wincing.

JACOB
He has bewitched me.

O'NEIL
Attend him, but have that hole dug all the faster.

O'Neil withdraws to his tent.

Whitehead looks back at Jacob, who is swigging from a wine bottle.

JACOB
Once I get my wind I shall smash every one of you bastards' teeth.

CUT TO:

Black.

Music.

WHITEHEAD V.O
Cough.

Jacob coughs V.O

WHITEHEAD V.O
Say 'arghhhh'

JACOB
Argggggh.

CUT TO:

EXT. FIELD - CAMPFIRE - DAY.

Tableau vivant: Cutler sits facing the hole. In front of him is the campfire, with another pot of bubbling stew.

Jacob stands by the fire, legs akimbo, hands on hips, his trousers dropped, his arse exposed to camera.

Between his legs we see Whitehead crouched with small magnifying glass to his eye, apparently studying Jacob's cock.

Friend digs the hole alone, whistling, in the distance. He has made good progress and is almost shoulder deep.

JACOB
Am I bewitched?

WHITEHEAD
(TIRED.)
No, sir. You merely suffer a disease in the private parts, occasioned by too much venereal sport.

CUT TO:

Cutler cuts mushrooms with a large knife, his musket balanced over his knees. He is methodically throwing the fungus into the pot as he listens.

CUT TO:

JACOB
(DISAPPOINTED.)
'Tis all?

WHITEHEAD
I also deduce Gout, Bloody Flux, Apostem of the Mouth, The pissing disease, St. Anthony's fire, Illiac-Passion, Hemorroids and Palsy brought on by drink.

JACOB
Then I am not turning into a frog?

WHITEHEAD
'Tis the one complaint you do not suffer, besides plague.

CUTLER
Back to work.

WHITEHEAD
All I can do is administer this poultice to your yard, to soothe.

Whitehead holds up a poultice of bound herbs.

CUT TO:

Jacob takes it, thoughtfully.

JACOB
(GENTLE.)
Thankyou.

Jacob shoves the poultice down his trousers.

Black.

We hear the sound of shovels digging.

The sound of labouring men.

JACOB V.O
I am my own man. I am my own man.

CUT TO:

EXT. FIELD - HOLE - DAY.

Jacob, Friend and Whitehead dig.

They are covered in mud.

JACOB V.O (CONT'D)
(DIGGING/ EXERTION/ ADAMANT.)
I. Am. My Own. Man.

Whitehead stops, swigs from a bottle of wine. Wipes his brow.

CUT TO:

EXT. FIELD - HOLE - DAY.

Cutler watches them all with gun poised.

Whitehead puts his hands together in prayer.

CUT TO:

EXT. FIELD - HOLE - DAY.

Whitehead prays.

WHITEHEAD
Please.

CUT TO:

Jacob digs.

JACOB
I am my own…

CUT TO:

WHITEHEAD
God.

CUT TO:

Friend digs like a machine.

CUT TO:

Whitehead, hands grasped in prayer.

WHITEHEAD
Save and deliver us; we humbly beseech thee, from the hands of your enemies; abate their pride, aswage their malice, confound their devices; that we, being armed with thy defence, may be preserved evermore from all perils, to glorify thee, who art only giver of all victory; through the merits of thy son, Jesus Christ, our Lord. Amen

Whitehead stops praying and looks up at the sky slowly.

Music.

CUT TO:

Above there is a large black dot hanging above Whitehead's head in the sky.

Whitehead looks back down and around at the other men in a dreamlike way.

They are all focused on something other.

CUT TO:

Jacob digs.

JACOB
I am my own man.

CUT TO:

Cutler cutting mushrooms.

CUT TO:

Friend scratching at the earth with his fingers; he unearths a clay piper, like the one Cutler stole from his pocket.

EXT. FIELD - CAMPFIRE - DAY.

Whitehead continues to gaze up at the black orb that no one else sees.

He climbs up the side of the hole.

JACOB
I am my own man.

CUT TO:

Whitehead walks towards O'Neil's tent.

JACOB V.O (CONT'D)
I am my own man.

CUT TO:

Cutler is preoccupied with the cross section of a mushroom that he holds close to his own face.

EXT. FIELD - HOLE - DAY.

Friend stops digging and considers his side of the hole, which is neat and tidy, with satisfaction.

FRIEND
Well, this is a fine hole we've dug here, that's for certain. The devil has to give us that. What do you say?

CUT TO:

EXT. FIELD - CAMPSITE - DAY.

Whitehead stands with his nose to the canvas of O'Neil's tent flap, breathing heavily.

Whitehead mouths the following dialogue, although the dialogue is spoken by Jacob.

JACOB V.O
I am my own-

CUT TO:

INT. THE TENT - DAY.

It is very dark.

O'Neil looks at himself in the scrying mirror.

In it is an inverted reflection of Whitehead from the end of the film, dressed in final clothes.

The 12 stones from Whitehead's stomach, which are laid out of the table, begin to glow, increasing the light cast on O'Neil's face.

O'Neil mouths the following dialogue, although the dialogue is spoken by Jacob.

WHITEHEAD V.O
Man.

CUT TO:

EXT. FIELD - HOLE - DAY.

Jacob, enraged by Friend's cheerful satisfaction, leaps on him roaring.

JACOB
(RAGE.)
You dumb bastard!

CUT TO:

EXT. FIELD - CAMPSITE - DAY.

Cutler drops the mushroom into the cook pot, leaps up, gun raised, and strides to the edge of the hole.

CUT TO:

Jacob and Friend are fighting like two bears in a pit.

JACOB
(SHOUTING.)
You are a slave!

FRIEND
(SHOUTING.)
And I shall be a better slave than you!

CUT TO:

Jacob punches Friend in the nose.

Friend digs his shovel into Jacob's foot.

Jacob howls.

JACOB
Fuuuuuuuuu

CUT TO:

EXT. FIELD - CAMPSITE - DAY.

O'Neil opens the tent flap, suddenly, coming nose to nose with Whitehead.

JACOB V.O (CONT'D)
uuuuuuuuuuuuck!

O'Neil smiles intimidatingly at Whitehead.

O'NEIL
Girding the loins?

WHITEHEAD
If you do not cease we may be blasted by an ill planet.

CUT TO:

EXT. FIELD - HOLE - DAY.

Cutler, having unleashed his cock, is pissing on Jacob and Friend. His gun and cock point in the same direction.

CUTLER
This is what a yard looks like, friend!

JACOB V.O
Argghhhhhhhh!

Jacob starts scrabbling up the side of the hole.

CUT TO:

EXT. FIELD - CAMPSITE - DAY.

O'Neil is distracted by unfolding events at the hole, moves away from Whitehead.

EXT. FIELD - HOLE - DAY.

Jacob grabs for Cutler.

JACOB
Argggghhhhhh!

Cutler fires clumsily at Jacob.

CUT TO:

Friend is shot.

He falls back against the wall of the hole.

CUT TO:

EXT. FIELD - HOLE - DAY.

Whitehead joins O'Neil, Jacob and Cutler, who stand at the edge of the hole looking down at Friend.

EXT. FIELD - HOLE - DAY.

Jacob jumps down in the hole.

JACOB
Friend?!

Friend is laid on his back, panting heavily.

Jacob grabs Friend roughly by the shoulders.

Tears spring to Jacob's eyes.

JACOB
Friend?!

The large wound is clearly evident on Friend's chest. The blood spreads across his shirt.

FRIEND
(TO JACOB.)
There, see?

Friend pales, sags, smiles.

FRIEND (CONT'D)
(TO JACOB.)

The word sounds good on your lips. The other fella uses it like a poking stick, does he not?

CUT TO:

Jacob looks back at Cutler with black hatred.

O'NEIL
(IRRITATED.)
What have you done, Cutler?

Whitehead jumps into the hole and examines Friend's chest.

Cutler looks belligerently unapologetic but shifty.

CUT TO:

FRIEND
(TO WHITEHEAD.)
I never had so many friend's as I do in this field.

Jacob looks with anguish to Whitehead.

JACOB
(INSISTENT/ DEMANDING.)
You can do something.

Whitehead, grips his jaw tightly and shakes his head, no.

Jacob vibrates with impotent rage.

CUT TO:

FRIEND
(TO WHITEHEAD.)
Remember my song.

Whitehead nods and looks coldly up at O'Neil and Cutler.

CUT TO:

FRIEND (CONT'D)
(TO JACOB.)
When you get to the ale house, see a way to send a message to my wife?

JACOB
Anything, friend. Anything.

Jacob gritting his teeth through tears of rage and guilt.

FRIEND
…Tell her…

Friend winces.

Jacob draws closer.

FRIEND (CONT'D)
…tell her I hate her.

Whitehead looks at Jacob uncertainly.

CUT TO:

Cutler and O'Neil draw in closer with unexpected interest.

CUT TO:

FRIEND (CONT'D)
Tell her I *did* burn her father's barn. T'was payment for forcing our marriage. Tell her I loved her sister. Who I had. Many times. From behind. Like a beautiful prize sow.

JACOB
(TO FRIEND/INCONSOLABLE.)
If I'd have known, I would have paid you more respect, brother.

Friend holds up a quieting hand.

FRIEND
And-

WHITEHEAD/JACOB
(TOGETHER.)
Yes?

FRIEND
lo… T'was good.

A great calm descends on Friend, having revealed the truth.

Friend dies with a satisfied smile on his face.

CUT TO:

Jacob sits back on his heels and weeps openly like a baby.

WHITEHEAD
(FURROWED BROW.)
I am the resurrection and the life, saith the Lord.

EXT. FIELD - CAMPSITE - DAY.

Cutler walks away.

WHITEHEAD V.O (CONT'D)
He that believeth in me, though he be dead, yet shall he live

EXT. FIELD - CAMPFIRE - DAY.

Cutler slumps by the fire and starts priming his gun like a grumpy teenager.

WHITEHEAD V.O (CONT'D)
And whosoever liveth and believeth in me shall never die.

EXT. FIELD - HOLE - DAY.

Whitehead and Jacob in the hole.

JACOB
Amen.

CUT TO:

O'Neil looks down with irritation, along the barrel of his gun, as if at a pair of ants. As soon as he begins to speak, Whitehead looks up.

O'NEIL
(BUSINESSLIKE.)
He has dug his grave but will not lay in it until that treasure is out. Deposit the corpse elsewhere for now.

CUT TO:

O'Neil walks over to Cutler.

CUT TO:

EXT. FIELD - HOLE - DAY.

Whitehead grasps Jacob's shoulder. A gesture of comfort, which is not rejected.

WHITEHEAD
He will have a Christian burial. No one will molest his bones.

Jacob nods, comforted, but weeps openly.

JACOB
(WISTFUL.)
I once had a sow.

Whitehead looks uncertain, but comforts Jacob anyway.

CUT TO:

EXT. FIELD - CAMPFIRE - DAY.

O'Neil looks on Cutler like an errant schoolboy.

CUTLER
He did it to himself.

O'Neil throws a shovel at Cutler with more than a little force.

O'NEIL
Down is the only way out for you, Cutler.

CUTLER looks at the shovel.

Black.

The sound of digging.

WHITEHEAD V.O
(SINGING.)
Baloo, my boy, lie still and sleep

It grieves me sore to hear thee weep

If thou'lt be silent I'll be glad

Thy moaning makes my heart full sad.

EXT. FIELD - HOLE - DAY.

Cutler is covered in mud.

WHITEHEAD V.O (CONT'D)
(SINGING.)
Baloo, my boy, thy mother's joy

Thy father bred me great annoy

Baloo, baloo, baloo, baloo

Baloo, baloo, lu-li-li-lu.

He digs, with feverish rage.

CUTLER
(TO HIMSELF/MISERABLE.)
Sooner I get back to fucking London, the fucking better. A new fucking coat. A fucking bed. Fucking doors to fucking shut. Citizens that make small fucking reckoning of Astrology.

CUT TO:

EXT. FIELD - CAMPSITE - DAY.

Jacob is slumped by the empty bottles, swigging the last mouth full of wine from the last full bottle.

WHITEHEAD V.O
(SINGING.)
Baloo, my boy, thy mother's joy

Thy father bred me great annoy

Baloo, baloo, baloo, baloo

Baloo, baloo, lu-li-li-lu.

The sound of Cutler's digging.

JACOB
(TO HIMSELF/MUTTERING.)
Truth be told I do not believe there is either God or Devil.

EXT. FIELD - DAY.

Whitehead drags Friend's corpse by the ankles, which are tied together with rope.

WHITEHEAD
(SINGING.)
O'er thee I keep my lonely watch

Intent thy lightest breath to catch

O, when thou wak'st to see thee smile.

We see that Friend's face is bound by a shirt.
His arms stretch out behind him, fingers threading through the long grass. They reach out as if trying to catch something he has lost.

EXT. FIELD - CAMPSITE - DAY.

Jacob looks over at O'Neil speculatively.

O'Neil can be seen through the open flap of the tent, obsessing over the stones from Whitehead stomach.
O'Neil's gun is lent against his table in an absent fashion.

JACOB
(TO HIMSELF/MUTTERING.)
Neither will I believe anything other than what I see. And what I see is two tits in a pantomime horse.

Jacob gets up, looks over at Cutler and takes a final swig of wine before throwing the last bottle onto the mound of empty bottles.

CUT TO:

Cutler digs.

CUTLER
(TO HIMSELF/ MISERABLE.)
I'd rather die of fucking plague in the fucking fleet than spend one more fucking minute in the fucking countryside.

CUT TO:

Jacob spits on the ground.

JACOB
(TO HIMSELF.)
I'll deliver that message, friend, if it be the last thing I do.

Jacob stumbles off unnoticed into the field, staggering blindly into the sun.

WHITEHEAD V.O
(SINGING.)
And thus my sorrow to beguile.

Baloo, my boy, thy mother's joy

Thy father bred me great annoy

Baloo, my boy, lie still and sleep

It grieves me sore to hear thee weep…

EXT. FIELD - DAY.

Whitehead comes to a place in the grass that he thinks appropriate to leave Friend.

WHITEHEAD V.O (CONT'D)
(SINGING.)
Twelve weary months have crept away

Since he, upon thy natal day

Left thee and me, to seek afar

He stops pulling, exhausted.

EXT. FIELD - FRIEND'S PLACE - DAY.

Whitehead slowly arranging Friend's limbs in a more orderly fashion, with great gentleness sings to him as he does. He picks clumps of grass and covers Friend, as if with a blanket.

WHITEHEAD (CONT'D)
(SINGING.)
A bloody fate in doubtful war.

Baloo, my boy, lie still and sleep

It grieves me sore to hear thee weep

If thou'lt be silent, I'll be glad

Thy moaning makes my heart full sad…

EXT. FIELD - DAY.

Jacob stumbles towards the far hedge, in which direction Cutler had originally indicated the ale house lay.

We see his feet drag through the grass.

WHITEHEAD V.O (CONT'D)
(SINGING.)
I dreamed a dream but yesternight

Thy father slain in foreign fight

He, wounded, stood beside my bed

His blood ran down upon thy head

He spoke no word, but looked on me

EXT. FIELD - HOLE - DAY.

Cutler's shovel hits something hard.

The sound that emanates is deep like a large Tibetan singing bowl or gong. (The sound from herein with be referred to as: 'Field Sound'.)

WHITEHEAD V.O (CONT'D)
(SINGING.)
Bent low, and gave a kiss to thee!

Baloo, baloo, my darling boy

Thou'rt now alone thy mother's joy.

CUTLER
(SHOUTING.)
Sir!

Cutler looks towards the tent with an expression of uncharacteristic excitement.

CUT TO:

INT. TENT - DAY.

O'Neil looks up with irritation as the sound reaches him.

CUTLER V.O
(SHOUTING.)
Sir!

EXT. FIELD - FRIEND'S PLACE - DAY.

Whitehead is laid down on his back next to Friend's corpse.

His eyes slowly close as if he is drifting into sleep.

Friend appears to be nothing more than a mound of grass now.

EXT. FIELD - HOLE - DAY.

O'Neil strides to the edge of the hole.

O'NEIL
(ANGRY.)
Christ in heaven, Cutler, where are they?!

Cutler, ecstatic. The most animated he has ever been.

CUTLER
We have it, sir. We have the treasure.

O'Neil looks mildly astonished.

O'NEIL
I must locate Whitehead.

CUTLER
Can we go to that ale house first, sir?

O'NEIL
Christ, Cutler, you grow dimmer by the minute. There is no damned ale house. T'was a figment of your imagination, what there is of it, to entice the digging drunk and the idiot.

Cutler looks perplexed.

CUTLER
Was it, sir?

O'NEIL
Well, dig it up man. Whitehead is worth more than this haul. I shall have him divining treasure across the land. I must capture him before he has a chance to start thinking for himself.

CUT TO:

O'Neil stalks off.

Cutler considers this last statement, before addressing O'Neil's back.

CUTLER
Do you not mean 'we' shall have him, sir?

CUT TO:

Black.

Music.

EXT. FIELD - FRIEND'S PLACE - DAY.

Whitehead slowly opens his eyes and looks at the large black ball floating close to the tip of his nose.

The 'Field Sound' sends its deep resonant call out to Whitehead.

CUT TO:

Jacob comes to the inner edge of the mushroom circle and stops abruptly. He feels unable to go any further.

Jacob drops to his knees.

The 'Field Sound' sends its deep resonant call out to Jacob.

CUT TO:

O'Neil strides through the field.

O'NEIL
Whitehead!

CUT TO:

Whitehead looks sideways into the field.

O'NEIL V.O (CONT'D)
Where are you coward?

Whitehead's focus shifts.

O'NEIL V.O (CONT'D)
Come to your master.

Whitehead looks back up at the sky and the black orb is gone.

WHITEHEAD
(TO HIMSELF.)
I am my own master.

CUT TO:

O'Neil stops, listens.

O'Neil continues striding on through the grass. He is facing in the opposite direction and some way off from Whitehead.

CUT TO:

EXT. FIELD - HOLE - DAY.

Cutler scratches at the earth with his hands, a glimpse of something is revealed. A long muddy shaft-

CUT TO:

EXT. FIELD - OPEN GROUND - DAY.

O'Neil lets off a shot.

We see it's result skitter through the grass.

EXT. FIELD - FAR HEDGE - DAY.

Jacob hears the crack of O'Neil's guns discharging and drops to the ground instantaneously.

JACOB
Whore of Babylon.

He pulls out the poultice from his trousers, looks at it, sniffs it and thinks.

CUT TO:

EXT. FIELD - HOLE - DAY.

Cutler stops for a beat, then continues scratching at the earth.

CUT TO:

EXT. FIELD - DAY.

O'Neil looks around and slumps to the ground to reload.

O'NEIL
(SHOUTING.)
You cannot escape the field.

CUT TO:

Whitehead shuffles along through the grass away from O'Neil on his belly.
Whitehead twists in the grass and comes face to face with the inner edge of the mushroom ring.

There are mushrooms all around him.

WHITEHEAD
(SHOUTING.)
Then I shall become it.

CUT TO:

O'Neil swings around and around looking blindly at the empty field, trying to discern in which vicinity Whitehead is concealed.

WHITEHEAD V.O (CONT'D)
(SHOUTING.)
And consume all the ill fortune which you are set to unleash.

CUT TO:

Whitehead picks a mushroom.

WHITEHEAD (CONT'D)
I shall chew up all the selfish scheming and ill intentions that men like you force upon men like me and bury it in the stomach of this place.

CUT TO:

Jacob stops.

JACOB
(TO HIMSELF.)
Christ in heaven. Stop speechifying, man, before he blows your ears off.

Jacob changes course towards Whitehead.

CUT TO:

O'Neil takes from his pocket a hand full of the stones which Whitehead previously threw up.

He chooses one at random and swallows it with difficulty.

O'NEIL
(SHOUTING.)
We are brothers, Whitehead.

CUT TO:

EXT. FIELD - HOLE - DAY.

Cutler uses his hands to revealed a broader expanse of something that is the open jaw of a skull.

CUTLER
Open up, you stubborn bastard.

CUT TO:

Whitehead opens his mouth and pops the mushroom in.

O'NEIL V.O
We are two halves of the same man!

CUT TO:

O'Neil speaks to the field...

O'NEIL (CONT'D)
You shall have as many books and lace bobbins as you like.

EXT. FIELD - HOLE - DAY.

Cutler gives up his excavations…

CUTLER
Fuck this.

CUT TO

Cutler scrambles up the side of the hole and pulls the pistol from his belt.

O'NEIL V.O
The country is at the edge of something, Whitehead.

EXT. FIELD - DAY. 72

Whitehead fills his mouth with mushrooms.

O'NEIL
Sever your conscience from your art and you will profit.

EXT. FIELD - HOLE - DAY.

Cutler stands on the edge of the hole and prepares to fire into it, aiming at the bottom of the hole.

CUT TO:

EXT. FIELD - DAY.

Whitehead crams more mushroom into his mouth.

EXT. FIELD - HOLE - DAY.

Cutler turns his head away.

EXT. FIELD - DAY.

Whitehead crams more mushroom into his mouth. (Each time the action becomes sped up and Whitehead more bug eyed.)

CUT TO:

EXT. FIELD - HOLE - DAY.

Cutler fires his gun at the hole.

Gun shot, musket flare, smoke.

Cutler is thrown backwards with great force onto the dirt pile.

EXT. FIELD - DAY.

Whitehead smiles broadly for the first time.

CUT TO:

EXT. FIELD - DAY.

Jacob is hit by a great wind blowing through the field. He struggles to continue forward.

(The wind may be silent and the following dialogue my be shouted by the actors over the wind, but then recorded later as whispered speech. The decision of the director.)

CUT TO:

EXT. FIELD - HOLE - DAY.

Stunned, Cutler puts his hand to his ear. He draws his hand away, finds his fingers covered in black blood.

Cutler bleeds from both ears.

CUT TO:

EXT. FIELD - DAY.

A great wind blows through the grass.

O'Neil staggers and is blown over, he prepares his gun with difficultly.

CUT TO:

EXT. FIELD - HOLE - DAY.

Cutler staggers off away from the hole.

As Cutler stumbled he stands on O'Neil's scrying mirror, breaking it in two.

CUT TO:

EXT. FIELD - DAY.

Whitehead pulls himself up against the wind.

EXT. FIELD - CAMPSITE - DAY.

O'Neil's tent is blown inside out.

It is carried up on the wind.

Books and papers toss and tumble and flap about like a wounded flock of birds.

Whitehead watches it in wonder.

CUT TO:

Through Whitehead's eyes the tent is transforms into a jerking, origami angel/demon/spirit, which dances on the wind.

A gun shot explodes.

JACOB V.O
Get down, you fool!

CUT TO:

EXT. FIELD - DAY.

Jacob pulls Whitehead down into the grass.

Another gunshot rings out.

JACOB (CONT'D)
I have come back to rescue you, you great dunderhead.

Whitehead looks around at Jacob and smiles.

WHITEHEAD
No, friend, it is I who will rescue you.

Whitehead points at the dancing tent.

WHITEHEAD
(SHOUTING/ MUTE/ WHISPERED)
Look. An angel. Mounting guard over the field's treasure.

CUT TO:

Jacob looks where Whitehead looks.

CUT TO:

All Jacob sees is a grubby old tent deflating on the ground.

CUT TO:

Jacob looks down at Whitehead's hands, which are full of mushrooms.

Jacob rolls his eyes.

Jacob, slaps the mushrooms from Whitehead's hands.

Jacob slaps Whitehead around the face.

Whitehead staggers.

Jacob grabs hold of Whitehead's arm preventing him from falling back.

JACOB
(SHOUTING/ MUTE/ WHISPERED)
I'll finish that bastard Cutler with my bare hands if I have to. You think of something to do with the Irish man.

Whitehead, bug-eyed, nods.

CUT TO:

Whitehead arranging himself on his knees and puts his hands together in prayer.

Jacob pulls Whitehead down low again.

JACOB (CONT'D)
(SHOUTING/ MUTE/ WHISPERED)
What are you doing?

WHITEHEAD
(SHOUTING/ MUTE/ WHISPERED)
Praying for his destruction.

Jacob is visibly irritated yet unnerved.

JACOB
Come, friend. I will protect you from yourself as best I can.

Jacob pushes Whitehead in front of him.

CUT TO:

Whitehead progresses through the grass on his hands and knees. His eyes wide, his hands and knees moving him in an unnatural fashion, like a giant insect.

CUT TO:

Whitehead, POV of the microscopic world of weevil, scuttling along his own path on his own mission.

WHITEHEAD
And after that I shall pray for more legs and arms, to greater appreciate the many natural intrigues and wonders that play out below us.

CUT TO:

Jacob looks up over the top of the grass and sees Cutler join O'Neil, and ducks back down quickly.

JACOB
Arses.

WHITEHEAD
Maybe I shall pen a book on the subject.

JACOB
We've less than no chance now they're together.

WHITEHEAD
What say you to this for a title? 'A Field in England or The Myriad Particulars of the Common Weevil.'

JACOB
Catchy.

WHITEHEAD
I shall beg Master Culpeper's advice at the first opportunity.

CUT TO:

EXT. FIELD - DAY.

Cutler and O'Neil battle to stand against the wind.

CUTLER
(VINDICATED/ HAPPY.)
There is no gold, sir. Whitehead's a lying bastard, just like his man Trower said. Just like I thought. Nothing in that hole but dirt and old bones.

CUT TO:

EXT. FIELD - DAY.

Whitehead puts his hands together in prayer again, and mouths the next words, which are spoken by Cutler.

CUTLER V.O
You put your money on the wrong man, sir. He is more of a charlatan and a fraud than you.

CUT TO:

O'Neil's face sets with a cold grim fury, as he looks on Cutler.

CUT TO:

Cutler looks surprised, as if not expecting to have said what he just did.

CUTLER (CONT'D)
(BACK-PEDDLING.)
I mean to say-

Cutler shakes his head as his tongue twists.

CUTLER (CONT'D)
(FLUSTERED.)
I don't mean to say, sir. That is, I mean to say that you are-

CUT TO:

O'Neil holds up a hand to stop Cutler.

The occult symbols on his palm are now smudged.

CUT TO:

EXT. FIELD - DAY.

Jacob watches O'Neil turn his back on Cutler.

Cutler is clearly begging, but this dialogue is not audible.

O'Neil moves away a pace.

CUT TO:

EXT. FIELD - DAY.

Whitehead's mouth moves in urgent, muttered prayer.

CUT TO:

EXT. FIELD - DAY.

O'Neil turns back to look at Cutler. O'Neil mouths the following but with the voice of Whitehead…

WHITEHEAD V.O
Open up now and let the devil in.

CUT TO:

O'Neil's pistol is in Cutler's mouth.

CUT TO:

EXT. FIELD - DAY.

O'Neil's finger on the trigger as it pulls.

CUT TO:

EXT. FIELD - DAY.

Jacob watches O'Neil unceremoniously shoot the back of Cutler's head off through his mouth.

CUT TO:

EXT. FIELD - DAY.

Cutler's brain explodes out of the back of his head.

CUT TO:

EXT. FIELD - DAY.

Whitehead's expanding iris as he takes a deep and sudden inhalation.

CUT TO

EXT. FIELD - DAY.

(Possibly have the expelled matter from Cutler's head transform into something else. Petals, seeds, something of the field…)

CUT TO:

Cutler falls to the ground.

CUT TO:

EXT. FIELD - DAY.

Whitehead appears to inhale all of the wind in the field.

CUT TO:

EXT. FIELD - DAY.

The field is now incredibly still and silent.

CUT TO:

EXT. FIELD - DAY.

O'Neil looks down at Cutler, as he belts his pistol.

O'NEIL
(SHOUTING.)
Whitehead!

He nudges Cutler's corpse with his boot.

CUT TO:

EXT. FIELD - DAY.

Jacob watches O'Neil walking away from their position.

JACOB
(WHISPERING.)
He's the king of cold-hearted bastards, I'll give him that.

CUT TO:

EXT. FIELD - DAY.

O'Neil's grim barking face.

O'NEIL
(SHOUTING.)
Whitehead!

CUT TO:

EXT. FIELD - DAY.

Jacob looks around at Whitehead, who has ceased praying.

JACOB
(WHISPERING.)
Could do with more like him in the ranks. You alright, brother?

CUT TO:

Whitehead unclasps his hands from prayer and looks at his own opens palms.

CUT TO:

Whitehead's palms fill the frame.

The camera looks on them as if it is the eyes of the person they belong to.

Our fingers slowly release each other from their knotted grip.

The palms open like the pages of a book and are covered in black blood.

CUT TO:

Whitehead's POV of Jacob running, low, towards Cutler's corpse in slow motion.

CUT TO:

EXT. FIELD - DAY.

Jacob is hunched on the floor over Cutler's corpse.

CUT TO:

Jacob claims Cutler's weapons, remaining powder and shot.

CUT TO:

Whitehead slumps down to watch Cutler loading Cutler's pistol.

JACOB
(LOW TONE.)
There's not much left. Here.

Jacob hands Whitehead Cutler's second gun.

WHITEHEAD
(LOW TONE.)
I have no knowledge of weapons.

CUT TO:

EXT. FIELD - DAY.

O'Neil swings around and fires.

CUT TO:

EXT. FIELD - DAY.

Jacob stops pouring powder from the powder horn. A plume of muzzle smoke rises some way off.

O'NEIL V.O
(Shouting.)
Whitehead!

CUT TO:

EXT. FIELD - DAY.

Whitehead is transfixed by the gun in his hands, which seems to pulsate, as Jacob loads his weapon.

WHITEHEAD
It comes alive, does it not, in your hand?

JACOB
Pay heed.

Whitehead focuses on watching Jacob pour powder down the barrel of the gun.

CUT TO:

Jacob then takes a patched lead ball and shoves it down the barrel until it rests on top of the powder charge.

CUT TO:

Friend slowly leans into shot, over Jacob and Whitehead's hunched shoulders, to watch the process with equal gravity.

When Jacob completes the weapon's preparation…

FRIEND
That's a fine load you have rammed home and no mistake.

CUT TO:

Jacob is startled near out of his skin.

JACOB
Almighty God in heaven!

CUT TO:

Whitehead turns slowly to find Friend peering over his shoulder, as if it was expected.

WHITEHEAD
Friend.

JACOB
You are dead, man!

FRIEND
(WHISPERING.)
I believe the Devil has work for me to do.

CUT TO:

Friend stands abruptly and turns his head in O'Neil's direction as he cups his hands to his mouth and shouts…

FRIEND (CONT'D)
(SHOUTING.)
They are over here, devil.

CUT TO:

EXT. FIELD - DAY.

O'Neil's head turns sharply and he releases one of his weapons.

CUT TO:

EXT. FIELD - DAY.

Jacob lurches over and sweeps Friend down into the grass by grabbing his ankles and pulling his legs from under him.

JACOB
Accursed idiot.

CUT TO:

Another shot rings out and flies through the grass.

Jacob is shot in the side.
He twists and contorts.

JACOB (CONT'D)
(HISSING.)
Fuck!

CUT TO:

Jacob slumps back in the grass and fires his gun reflexively towards O'Neil's position.

CUT TO:

EXT. FIELD - DAY.

The shot cuts through the grass.

CUT TO:

EXT. FIELD - DAY.

The shot passes through O'Neil's calf bone. The splintering noise clearly audible.

He is mildly surprised.

He looks down at his leg, drenched in pumping blood.

He thinks for a moment, then lowers himself to the ground with an almost unrushed elegance.

His coat billowing out around him as his leg crumbles beneath him.

O'Neil blinks.

O'NEIL
(SHOUTING.)
You chose to associate with a low sort, Whitehead.

CUT TO:

EXT. FIELD - DAY.

Whitehead has Friend in a headlock, a hand clamped firmly over Friend's mouth. Friend struggles and mumbles loudly.

O'NEIL
(SHOUTING.)
Very well.

Whitehead looks to Jacob with grave concern.

WHITEHEAD
(WHISPERED.)
Perhaps Almighty God has chosen me for your personal physician. I shall attend you, presently, if this maniac will hold his tongue.

Jacob lobs the discharged gun at Whitehead. He is in extreme pain and struggles to retain his usual machismo.

JACOB
(WHISPERED.)
Attend that.

WHITEHEAD
(TO FRIEND.)
No, not utter a word, otherwise-

Whitehead is lost for words

JACOB
He will turn you into a weevil.

Whitehead lets go of Friend face.

FRIEND
I shall say but one thing. I have missed you both.

Whitehead begins to charge the gun, with clumsy but swift hands.

CUT TO:

EXT. FIELD - DAY.

O'Neil is crawling through the grass with difficulty, dragging his leg.

CUT TO:

EXT. FIELD - DAY.

Blood spurts from Jacob's side.

JACOB
(WHISPERED.)
We have few shot left.

Whitehead fumbles with the gun.

WHITEHEAD
(TO JACOB.)
You will die if I do not apply pressure.

Jacob kicks out at Friend.

JACOB
(WHISPERED.)
Then perhaps tis this bastard's turn to take a lesson from me. Christ in heaven, he has risen more times than Lazarus.

Jacob, fueled by pain and rage, grabs Friend by the throat.

JACOB (CONT'D)
Watch carefully as I die and take note of how to do it.

Friend struggling to breath.

JACOB (CONT'D)
(MOUNTING RAGE)
…I should deliver that message to your wife on the end of my cock.

Jacob releases Friend, who gasps, and begins to load another gun. This time his hands are not so swift.

Friend thinks and nurses his own neck.

FRIEND
Is that to say we are still friends?

Friend smiles a broad, winning smile full of hope.

Jacob stops loading his weapon for a moment, over come with exasperation.

JACOB.
(TO FRIEND/ ENRAGED/ LOUD)
No! We are not!

CUT TO:

EXT. FIELD - DAY.

O'Neil's lets off both of his guns.

CUT TO:

EXT. FIELD - DAY.

Two shots cut through the grass, just missing the boys.

CUT TO:

Whitehead holds his finger to his mouth in a quieting motion.

Friend's smile sinks.

Friend's brow furrows.

CUT TO:

EXT. FIELD - DAY.

O'Neil is swathed in a plume of smoke.

WHITEHEAD V.O

He is injured. He rests some 70 odd yards or so yonder.

CUT TO:

EXT. FIELD - DAY.

Jacob finishes loading the gun he is working at. His pain is great and growing.

JACOB

(STRAINED WHISPER.)

This is our last shot. You may still catch your quarry single-handed.

CUT TO:

Friend's expression is as if he has been shot through the heart by the growing intimacy between Whitehead and Jacob.

FRIEND
What about me?

CUT TO:

Whitehead focuses intently on Jacob, ignoring Friend.

CUT TO:

Jacob's shaking hand passes the gun to Whitehead.

Whitehead is now loaded with all remaining weapons.

Jacob looks on him like a proud father.

JACOB
There. *Now* you are a soldier.

Whitehead looks at Jacob, who bleeds heavily and becomes paler by the moment, with great sadness.

WHITEHEAD
(TO JACOB.)
I am no soldier.

JACOB
Will he find you running away?

WHITEHEAD
(RESOLUTE.)
He will not, sir. Not this time.

Whitehead and Jacob exchange a comradely look and a warm smile.

CUT TO:

Friend looks put out, as nobody smiles at him.

CUT TO:

Whitehead goes to leave.

JACOB
Hey.

Whitehead stops and turns back to Jacob.

JACOB (CONT'D)
…You think there is treasure in this field?

WHITEHEAD
The treasure is here between us, is it not, friend.

Jacob nods with pleasure.

Whitehead and Jacob join in a manly embrace, patting each other heavily on the back.

JACOB
A pretty sentiment. You will no doubt starve on your own.

CUT TO:

Jacob and Friend watch as Whitehead crawls out into the field alone.

CUT TO:

Jacob slumps back down.

JACOB
Nice bloke. I'd have liked to have shared that ale with him.

CUT TO:

Tears have sprung to Friend's eyes. His expression is one of a jilted lover.

FRIEND
(HEARTBROKEN.)
So. He is your better friend now. You two are as peas in a pod. And I am but to pick up the scraps of your affection.

Jacob rolls his eyes with utter perplexity and torture.

FRIEND (CONT'D)
No, do not speak. The message was clear in the way you embraced him. Well, I shall prove my worth as a better friend to you yet, see if I don't.

CUT TO:

Friend is up and away through the grass, quick as a rabbit.

CUT TO:

Two shots, ringing out from O'Neil's guns, dance at his heels.

CUT TO:

Jacob rolls his eyes again and slumps back into the grass, looking at the sky.

JACOB
(TO HIMSELF.)
Shit and thistles.

CUT TO:

Black.

Music (See 'The Battalia' from The Six Calls of War)

EXT. FIELD - SUNSET.

We see Whitehead's face, an expression of grim determination, as he snakes on his belly through the grass.

CUT TO:

Smoke gathers over the field in increasing density.

CUT TO:

Black.

The sound of Whitehead's breath.

CUT TO:

Whitehead crawls closer to O'Neil's position with the pistol in his belt and the musket parting the grass in front of him with slow careful determination.

CUT TO:

Black.

The sound of the grass.

EXT. FIELD - SUNSET.

O'Neil loading his weapon.

O'NEIL
(MUMBLING/ SINGING TO HIMSELF.)
Baloo, my boy, lie still and sleep

It grieves me sore to hear thee weep-

CUT TO:

Black.

The sound of a heart beating.

CUT TO:

EXT. FIELD - DAY.

Whitehead looks up over the dancing grass and sees the crown of O'Neil's head before it is swathed in a drift of smoke.

O'NEIL V.O (CONT'D)
(SINGING.)
O'er thee I keep my lonely watch

Intent thy lightest breath to catch

O, when thou wak'st to see thee-

Whitehead raises his pistol.

CUT TO:

O'Neil turns his head suddenly.

O'NEIL (CONT'D)
(TO HIMSELF.)
Damn. What is the rest of that song?

CUT TO:

Whitehead creeps closer still to O'Neil.

CUT TO:

Black.

The sound of Friend screaming like a banshee while runnings.

CUT TO:

Friend comes charging out of the smoke brandishing his broken pike at the camera.

CUT TO:

O'Neil, fumbling in surprise, shoots Friend dead, for the final time.

CUT TO:

O'Neil flinches back, falling into the grass shaken.

CUT TO:

Black.

WHITEHEAD V.O
(WHISPERED.)
The coward is here.

CUT TO:

Music.

Whitehead running POV as he approaches O'Neil from behind.

(O'Neil's head may be obscured by a black dot.)

CUT TO:

O'Neil stumbles to his feet, unaware of Whitehead's approach. He is moving towards Friend's body. All the time the black dot obscures his head.

CUT TO:

O'Neil turns at the sounds of Whitehead's footsteps.

O'Neil's POV of Whitehead running towards him, gun pointed.

Whitehead's head is also obscured by a black dot.

The black dot over Whitehead's head fills the screen as he nears

CUT TO:

Black.

The sound of a gunshot.

CUT TO:

Smoke drifts across the field.

The sound of a shovel digging.

CUT TO:

We see the bodies of Friend and Jacob at the bottom of the hole.

Whitehead is now dressed in O'Neil's coat.

He shovels soil into the hole to bury Jacob and Friend.

CUT TO:

Black.

The sound of worn boots trudging laboriously through mud.

CUT TO:

Whitehead sits by the campfire alone, with a gun.

He stirs the mushroom strew, adding unidentified lumps of raw meat and a handful of mushrooms.

His expression is businesslike.

He looks up as sounds of a distant battle draw near.

CUT TO:

Whitehead retrieves the Master's stolen documents from amongst the long grass, the broken halves of the scrying mirror, and the 12 stones. Four of the stones are bloodied.

Whitehead sets all these elements out carefully on the ground.

CUT TO:

Whitehead holds the two halves of the broken scrying mirror up to the sun.

The black circle in front of the sun mimics an eclipse.

CUT TO:

Black.

The sounds of exerted breath as someone walks at a slow steady pace.

EXT. FIELD - HEDGEROW - DAY.

The camera follows the course of a dense hedgerow along the edge of a fallow field, right to left.

Mud and shit predominate.
The air is thick with smoke.

We here musket shots being released in a quick volley from some near place on the other side of the hedge.

The sound of worn boots trudging stops abruptly, as does the camera.

The sound of running feet coming towards the hedgerow on the opposite side.

WHITEHEAD V.O
Friend?

The worn boots commence trudging again with a little more purpose as the camera follows the course of the dense hedgerow a little way back along left to right.

CUT TO:

Whitehead comes running up the hedgerow.

His back is presented to us as the following question is presented…

WHITEHEAD V.O (CONT'D)
Hey, Friend?

Whitehead looks around himself, but everywhere is thick with muzzle smoke.

Panting heavily, Whitehead drops his guns and pushes into the hedgerow.

CUT TO:

Black.

The sound of Whitehead struggling through the hedgerow.

CUT TO:

The camera follows the course of the hedgerow on the opposite side from Whitehead's entry.

It tries to locate the correct point at which White-head will emerge, by way of listening to his sounds of struggle and muttered oaths.

WHITEHEAD V.O (CONT'D)
What is your name, friend?

A little along, the hedge shakes like a jelly and the camera journeys there directly.

CUT TO:

The camera, on the far side of the hedgerow, watches Whitehead emerge from the hedge, hands first.

WHITEHEAD V.O (CONT'D)
Your name?

CUT TO:

Whitehead pulls himself free of the hedgerow. Torn, tattered, he brushes himself before he looks up and his eyes become full of shock and disbelief.

CUT TO:

Tableau vivant: Whitehead stands between Jacob and Friend.

All three men stand facing the camera as if captured in an engraving.

Music: drumming (see 'The Retreat' from The Six Calls to War

Finis

IN THE EARTH

PART 1

The Arrival

EXT. GANTALOW LODGE - DAY 1.

Rules on a board. Specific detail about keeping clean and the non transference of germs. ALL procedures must be followed.

Close up hand washing. Over and over. Thumbs, finger gaps, the full WHO.

Feet stepping into a tray of disinfectant. Sloshing about.

Gantalow Lodge. A purpose built hunting lodge. Empty since the pandemic and now under control of the government funded science body the Fashdale Institute.

Beyond is the Arboreal Forest. 250 sq. miles of wilderness. The biggest in the UK.

MARTIN (30), dressed in work trousers and a black waterproof jacket walks out of the hygiene area and is sprayed down by a hazmat-suited figure pumping a bottle of disinfectant.

Gantalow Lodge Owner Lord James KAREL (45) is standing twelve feet away. The distance is marked on the ground. He looks through some paper work.

KAREL (SHOUTING)
WELCOME! How is the town?

MARTIN (SHOUTING)
Quietening down now. I think. Food is arriving on time. I was only there a day, from the transit.

KAREL (SHOUTING)
That's good. Normal is what we want.

MARTIN(SHOUTING)
Bristol took it pretty hard after the third wave. It's under control now though.

Karel nods.

KAREL (SHOUTING)
This is Doctor Jarrek... He's handling the lock down procedures here.

He beckons to an older man who is approaching from the visitors centre. Dr. Frank JARREK (53) waves semi officially.

MARTIN
Doctor Jarrek. Martin Lowery.

JARREK
Doctor Lowery... welcome.

INT. JARREK'S MAKESHIFT SURGERY - DAY 1.

Karel and Jarrek are sat apart in the surgery. It's larger than normal to allow social distancing. Doctor Jarrek puts Martin through a series of tests. Blood work, heart rate. He pees in a cup.

KAREL
We've been closed for over a year now. I just want to get open again.

MARTIN
And you own it?

KAREL
Yes, well the woods are leased to the government during the crisis.

How many projects are the Fashdale Institute running here, Frank?

JARREK
Nine currently including this one.

KAREL
Usually this would be teeming with holiday makers. They are drawn to it from all over.

MARTIN
It's appreciated. We really couldn't do the research we are doing without your co-operation.

KAREL
Well, it's all for the good isn't. Fashdale Institute grants are keeping us going. Long may it last! What specifically are you working on?

MARTIN
Doctor Wendle's project? researching ways of making crops more efficient. Through the study of Mycorrhiza.

KAREL
That was it. Growths on roots? Forming networks? Funny place to do that, in a forest.

MARTIN
You have very special land here. It's unusually fertile.

Karel smiles and looks at Jarrek doing his job.

KAREL
Sorry about all this fuss.

MARTIN
I know it's a delicate ecosystem out here, you can't be too careful.

Karel doesn't look up.

KAREL
Mainly we don't want to get sick. Have you got any paper work for me?

Martin hands over his docket. Karel leafs through it. Scans a QAR code with his phone. He looks up darkly.

KAREL (CONT'D)
A couple of people died in the village. It brought it all home really.

He turns the soil sampler over in his gloved hands. It's about the size of a shoebox.

Martin signs it. Gives it back. He takes in the atmosphere for a moment.

MARTIN
It's quiet out here.

KAREL
That's how we like it.

They listen for a minute.

MARTIN
No cars.

INT. JARREK'S MAKESHIFT SURGERY - DAY 1.

Martin sits waiting for results.

He looks up and sees a woodcut of a robed figure with wooden horns. PARNAG FEGG it says in a wispy font.

ALMA Pesco enters the room.

ALMA
Hi, Dr. Lowery? I'm Alma. I'm guiding you out to ATU 327A. Doctor Wendle's site.

MARTIN
Please, it's Martin…

Alma moves over to the drinks station.

ALMA
Do you want one?

MARTIN
Thanks.

He watches how she makes it. She washes her hands up to the elbows. Boils water. Gets cups out. Always worried now about how clean things are.

ALMA
Have you got any coffee?

Martin smiles and pulls out a jar of instant.

ALMA (CONT'D)
Oh. Thank you. We haven't had any in months.

Alma smiles as she washes the jar. She looks over to where Martin is staring at the woodcut.

ALMA (CONT'D)
Worried she's going to get you?

Martin smiles.

MARTIN
Who is Parnag Fegg?

ALMA
It's a local folk tale, She's the spirit of the woods. She protects travelers, guiding people out of the woods if they are lost.

MARTIN
She looks quite intense.

ALMA
It's something to tell the kids. Stops them wandering off.

She hands Martin a coffee

ALMA (CONT'D)
They had a few go missing in the 70s. This helps make them a bit more aware.

MARTIN
But you don't believe it?

Alma shrugs.

ALMA
I'm not even sure how old this image is. It's just something they picked up with all the rest of the decoration in here. This stuff is all new. For tourists.

She looks out of the window for a minute, sipping her coffee.

ALMA (CONT'D)
I believe in the forest.

She looks at Martin. She can see it's not answered his question.

ALMA (CONT'D)
It's a living thing you can sense. I can see why people tried to give that feeling a face.

Martin looks at the grisly woodcut. Bodies are being dragged into a standing stone. A man and woman stand as if they are getting married.

MARTIN
Are you sure she helped people?

Alma looks at him.

ALMA
Martin Lowery. I'm sure I know that name from somewhere.

MARTIN
It's not an uncommon name. There was another Martin Lowery in my school.

ALMA
Really?

MARTIN
He hated me.

ALMA
That's odd.

MARTIN
He said I had his name and he punched me.

Martin laughs at the memory of it. Also that he looked him up on Facebook years later and his life seemed much worse than his own.

INT. GANTALOW LODGE - DAY 1.

Alma shows him to his room.

ALMA
We leave first thing in the morning.

MARTIN
How far is it?

ALMA
ATU 327A? It's 2 days on foot.

MARTIN
There's no other way?

ALMA
What like a bus or something?

MARTIN
(HOPEFULLY.)
or a quad bike…

ALMA
No, just a long walk.

INT. ROOM - DAY 1.

Martin goes through his equipment and supplies. He plugs in the soil sampler just to make sure it's working. It pings into life. He unplugs it and packs it away. He gets out his diary opens it and makes an entry into it.

There is a knock on the door. Doctor Jarrek.

Martin invites him in. Jarrek keeps his distance. He's holding Martin's results. He looks at the diary.

JARREK
It's good discipline, writing a diary.

Martin closes the diary from Jarrek's prying eyes.

JARREK (CONT'D)
I don't want you over-exerting yourself. The report said you have had ringworm recently.

MARTIN
Yes. I don't know where that came from.

JARREK
It's a pretty harmless fungus. Cleared up now?

MARTIN
About a week ago.

JARREK
How long have you been in isolation?

MARTIN
Four months. But I've been exercising.

Jarrek smiles. He can see Martin hasn't been from the medical.

JARREK
We had to send a rescue party in to get a group out a couple of months ago. They got lost. Thought they could find their way, went without a ranger. Panicked. Arrogant really.

MARTIN
They didn't use GPRS?

JARREK
Theres no reception in there.

MARTIN
Of course not.

JARREK
People get funny in the woods sometimes. Nerves.

Martin nods along. Taking it in… But not taking it on.

MARTIN
Sounds almost superstitious.

JARREK
People would do well to be afraid. It is a hostile environment.

EXT. GANTALOW LODGE - DAY 1

Martin watches the sun set. He goes back into his room. It doesn't look so hostile. He smiles. Happy to be out.

He sits down and gets out a letter. Inside is a photograph of a woman. His wife? Sweetheart? It's actually Doctor Wendle.
He turns it over in his hands.

EXT. GANTALOW LODGE - 5.30 MORNING. DAY 2.

Travel Alarm goes off. Martin hand washing. Coffee making. Martin gets himself together. Goes through his morning exercise regime… It's a bit half-hearted.

Alma is waiting outside. Smoking a roll-up.

Martin walks over to her carrying his rucksack and a smaller bag with the soil sampler in it.

ALMA
Is that it?

MARTIN
Yes.

Alma makes a "I could have taken that," followed by a "What's the fuss about?" face.

ALMA
Ok. You ready?

MARTIN
Sure.

Jarrek and Karel watch them from a window. Suspicious.

EXT. ROAD - DAY 2.

Alma and Martin walk along the road towards the woodland.

EXT. FIELD OF LONG GRASS - DAY 2.

Martin and Alma walk through the field as if wading through water.

EXT. FIELD BEFORE THE TREES - DAY 2.

Martin and Alma move through the more managed land towards the forest.

ALMA
Nobody has seen Doctor Wendle in six months.

Martin strains to understand.

ALMA (CONT'D)
We have had written notes. She leaves in drop boxes. But I haven't been near where she is camped in months.

On her request.

MARTIN
She likes the quiet.

ALMA
You know the doctor personally?

MARTIN
Yes. We worked closely together when she was at Harringdon Research Laboratories.

He pauses as he micro-remembers it.

MARTIN(CONT'D)
It was a few years ago now.
I moved on to another project.

Slight pause. Theres something here. Regret.

ALMA
And she asked for you to come out?

MARTIN
No. I requested.

ALMA
Not someone from her own team?

MARTIN
All the research groups at Fashdale are stretched a bit thin. I've worked with this soil sampler, and I know her research. So it made sense.

Alma takes the answer. Not entirely convinced.

EXT. FOREST - DAY 2.

Alma and Martin walk along a path in dappled light. Deeper into the forest.

ALMA
So what is really going on out there?

MARTIN
What do you mean?

ALMA
I know the official story, "soil testing"

Martin teasing.

MARTIN
Oh is this like a conspiracy?

ALMA
I've heard that it's something to do with the virus. That she is looking for a cure.

It's good if that's it.

MARTIN
Where did you hear that?

ALMA
People at the camp from other projects.

MARTIN
The Fashdale Institute is an agricultural research facility. We are not epidemiologists.

ALMA
I'm aware of that.

It goes quiet for a moment. Fallen at the first hurdle. Alma picks it back up.

ALMA (CONT'D)
I read her paper on Mycorrhiza.

Martin smiles. Alma smiles back.

MARTIN
It's a beautiful system. The plants as a network.

ALMA
When I first started working in the forest I thought it was more Darwinian. That the trees were in competition with each other for the light. But it makes much more sense that they work as a network. Supporting each other. The Mycorrhiza extending their roots and joining them together.

MARTIN
Yes.
We think we invented the internet… It was always here beneath our feet.

ALMA
And what is Doctor Wendle doing with it?

MARTIN
Trying to monitor it… to communicate with it, to find out what it needs.

ALMA
What they need is for us to leave them alone.

EXT. FOREST - DAY 2.

There is a rock with a splash of yellow paint on it. Alma stops at the marker.

Alma gets out her radio.

ALMA
Hello, Base. Sparrow here.

RADIO
Hello, Sparrow. How are you doing?

ALMA
Fine. Going out of contact. Back in a week.

We see a puffball fungus in the foreground. It puffs out a cloud of spores.

They walk on.

EXT. FOREST DAY - DAY 2.

Another rock. Painted blue.
She walks behind the marker and pulls out a Tupperware box from inside a rotten tree. She opens it.

Alma looks at the geo-cache. It's empty.

MARTIN
How long has it been since you have heard from Doctor Wendle?

ALMA
Two months now… Since the request for the soil sampler.

They start walking deeper into the Forest.

Martin listens for a moment. Hearing all sorts of tweeting. There is a very distinct sounding bird. Something that Martin has never heard before.

MARTIN
What is that?

ALMA
We have a lot of bird life that you don't hear in the rest of the country.

Martin smiles as he listens to the birds.

EXT. FOREST - EVENING - DAY 2.

Alma and Martin set up their tents. Eat food.

ALMA
I know where I know your name from.

MARTIN
Where?

ALMA
Letters that I picked up from Doctor Wendle. She wrote to you a lot.

MARTIN
We kept in correspondence.

ALMA
It was driving me mad. All last year. Then it stopped.

MARTIN
Yes.

Martin looks sad.

MARTIN (CONT'D)
Sometimes a conversation just runs it's course.

ALMA
I bet you are looking forward to seeing her again.

MARTIN
Yes. It's been a while now. With the isolation it's nice to see anybody.

ALMA
Even me!

MARTIN
Ha.

ALMA
I'm not so bothered. My work can be pretty remote. I like it like that.

They turn in for the night. Alma covers the fire.

Later in his tent Martin is aware of the forest. The calls of animals. The creaking of the ancient trees.

EXT. FOREST - DAY 3.

Alma and Martin pack up their tent and move off.

Alma has to check in on various drop boxes and recording sites.

She gathers information. Takes out memory cards and downloads info onto a rugged hard-drive.

The bits of equipment are covered in bind weed and other growths. Alma struggles slightly.

ALMA
SO much growth in the last few weeks.

Martin is leaning against a tree, happy to be stopped for a moment.

EXT. FOREST - DAY 3.

Martin follows behind Alma. She is picking up the pace now. His excitement about being outside is ebbing away with each step. He slogs on.

Soon Martin is worn out. He leans up against a tree.

MARTIN
How far have we walked?.

ALMA
Ten miles. Not much.

MARTIN
I'm exhausted.

Alma smiles.

ALMA
Walk through it. It will get better.

He eats a biscuit.

ALMA (CONT'D)
The next break is in about 20 mins. Come on. It's not that far.

He pulls himself up.

MARTIN
You are a torturer.

EXT. WOODS - DAY 3.

Martin slogs along. He is sweating and exhausted.

He looks ahead and sees Alma in the distance. Merri-ly yomping along without a care in the world.

MARTIN (SHOUTS)
I'm sorry for being so feeble. I lied to Dr. Jarrek.

I haven't been exercising. I've just been sitting around. I couldn't face it.

Alma not looking back.

ALMA
You'll get your breath.

MARTIN
I thought I would get lots done during the lockdown. But I just vegetated.

Alma smiles.

MARTIN (CONT'D)
I'm supposed to be a botanist. I killed every single plant in my flat.

EXT. FOREST - DAY 3.

Sitting in a clearing They have a tea. Martin catches his breath.

ALMA
It's good for you.

Martin sneezes.

MARTIN
Then why do I feel so awful?

Alma looks worried for a moment. The shadow of the virus is always there.

ALMA
Allergies?

MARTIN
I don't get them. At least used to.

EXT. FOREST - DAY 3.

They move on deep in the forest now.

Alma sees something. A tiny scrap of paper. A chocolate wrapper. She pokes at it with a stick.

ALMA
Odd.

MARTIN
It could have blown in.

She thinks for a moment.

ALMA
People come and live in the woods, we have had trouble with it in the past.

MARTIN
Who would do that?

ALMA
My parents lived off grid for years. Traveling all over.
Following the road protests. They would camp in trees, live in caves. Anywhere.

MARTIN
Mine worked at the council. I don't think they ever went camping. They hated it.

ALMA
It's a hard life. They gave up on it in the end. Settled in London. Got proper jobs.

MARTIN
Is that why you ended up as a Ranger, to return to the woods?

ALMA
I didn't end up as anything. I chose this. I was working as an Engineer. I retrained. I'd had enough of indoors.

She sees a broken branch. She looks around. Broken Bracken. She walks off the path. Martin follows.

MARTIN
Where are you going?

ALMA
I need to have a look at something. You stay here.

MARTIN
Why?

ALMA
You make too much noise.

Then she moves off.

MARTIN
Fine.

Martin watches her go into the woods. Puffs out his cheeks. He sits down exhausted.

Then he hears a noise. A crack of wood.

MARTIN (CONT'D)
Hello?

He peers out into the forest. He sees a figure moving… a way off between the trees.

MARTIN (CONT'D)
HELLO!

He gets up and moves towards the figure. Wading into the undergrowth.

MARTIN (CONT'D)
HELLO THERE!

He takes a few more steps then looks around. Stops. The figure is gone. He listens to the birdsong for a moment. Happy to be outside.

Looking around he frowns. Everything looks very similar. He turns again. No. Nothing familiar.

MARTIN (CONT'D)
I came in here… turned. And back there…

He walks on a bit. Then stops. It comes upon him in a sickening wave.

He is lost.

MARTIN (CONT'D)
No no no no…

He walks back… Re-tracing his steps… It's no good.. He stops.

MARTIN (CONT'D)
I turned right then left. Down the path… so… The sun was… fuck…

He walks back… But no. He is totally lost. He looks off across a valley of trees. Forest stretching off in all directions.

MARTIN (CONT'D)
Fuck.

He walks on.

MARTIN (CONT'D)
ALMA!

He sits down exhausted. He eats a snack. He hits his head with his fist.

MARTIN (CONT'D)
STUPID STUPID.

ALMA
What are you doing?

Martin looks up shocked.

MARTIN
I thought I saw someone…

Alma Frowns

ALMA
I told you to stay there.

MARTIN
I'm sorry.

ALMA
Who did you see? A family?

MARTIN
No.

Martin thinks for a minute.

MARTIN (CONT'D)
It must have been the light… Where did you go?

EXT. FOREST - DAY 3.

Alma leads him to an abandoned camp site… A brightly coloured family tent flapping in the breeze. Alma turns over a sodden book with a twig.

ALMA
They have gone… in a hurry. There's food here.

She finds a toy and frowns.

MARTIN
Why would they leave these things?

ALMA
I found a camp like this before… a family. They came out here, and got sick… No one could save them.

MARTIN
They died?

ALMA
People do desperate things in extreme situations. You find out who you really are quickly.

Alma drifts off into dark thoughts and turns away. Martin pulls a face trying to process what she has just said. Fuck.
He breathes in the air, trying to lighten the atmosphere.

MARTIN
How far are we from Dr. Wendle's camp?

ALMA
About 15 miles.

MARTIN
Then we are already on top of it

ALMA
What?

MARTIN
The Mychorrizal mat. All these trees are connected and controlled by it.

Alma sees a splatter of blood on the side of the tent. She frowns.

ALMA
In her paper Doctor Wendle made it sound like a brain.

MARTIN
Yes. I suppose it is.

Alma smiles curtly. Hiding the truth from Martin. She is already worried about him, He doesn't need this to think about as well.

ALMA
Lets go.

EXT. FOREST - DAY 3.

Alma disappears into the woods as Martin tries to keep up. Suddenly he sees a man-made structure. Iron railings around a plinth. He looks up to see a column some 300ft tall with an urn at the top. He sees Alma ahead throwing down her bags

MARTIN
What is it?

ALMA
It's a folly. Built by Lord Barrings in 1850 to commemorate the death of his wife.

MARTIN
I'm impressed by your knowledge.

ALMA
It's written on the side.

MARTIN
What is it doing out here?

ALMA
This was their spot apparently.

MARTIN
It's quite romantic.

ALMA
I hate it. She's dead, she doesn't care. He has just come out here and put up this big stone cock in the landscape.

MARTIN
That's one way of looking at it.

ALMA
Yeah. I am looking at it and it's hurting my eyes.

Martin looks out across the valley and sees the woods stretchin on for miles.

EXT. FOREST - EVENING - DAY 3.

They set up a camp. Two one-man tents. A fire. Martin is lost in thought.

She looks at him in the firelight. He looks back.

MARTIN
What?

ALMA
You looked like you were a million miles away.

MARTIN
It's odd being outside for the first time in months. It's hard to take in.

ALMA
Things will get back to normal quicker than you think. Everyone will forget what happened.

MARTIN
I don't think anyone will forget.

ALMA
They will. They will be back to their old ways.

Why did you leave the Harringdon facility?

Martin snapping out of the moment…

MARTIN
What?

ALMA
Before you said you worked with Doctor Wendle at the Harringdon facility. Why did you leave?

MARTIN
Personal reasons.

They see something in the distance and hear a noise.

A deep throbbing noise that seems to rise up then drop down again. Then what looks like lightning in the woods. flashing.

The sound rises with the pulsing light

MARTIN (CONT'D)
Is that where the doctor's camp is?

ALMA
Yes.

Martin looks worried.

ALMA (CONT'D)
What is she doing out there?

Martin tries to formulate an idea but can't.

MARTIN
I don't know.

ALMA
Well she can tell us in the morning.

INT. TENT - NIGHT - DAY 3.

Martin lays in his tent. He can hear the throbbing noise. It's far away but consistent.
He pulls up his sleeve and looks at his ringworm. It's back now, spreading. Somehow aggravated by being outside. He rubs cream into it.
He drifts off. Darkness. Then he hears a voice and there's a tapping.

ALMA (OUTSIDE)
Wake up.

Martin pokes his head out of his tent.

MARTIN
What is it?

Martin blinks at the tree line.

ALMA
Something's there.

MARTIN
What, an animal?

They are both quiet for a moment. Just breathing and trees creaking.

ALMA
I don't know.

Alma shines her torch into the woods. There is nothing. She stands for a moment. Then goes back to her tent.

MARTIN
What could it be?

ALMA
Wolves.

Martin panics a bit.

MARTIN
There are wolves here?

ALMA
Yes and bears. It's been re-wilded. They sniff around for food. They are mostly harmless.

MARTIN
Are you saying that so I can get back to sleep?

ALMA
They haven't mauled anyone in years.

Martin settles in and tries to go to sleep.

MARTIN
Jesus.

He drifts off.

INT. TENT - NIGHT - DAY 3.

Silence. Trees creak. Then the noise again.

The throbbing thud of bass followed by howls of high frequency. A mournful sound like whale song.

Then it stops. He goes back to sleep. Black.
Wind blowing.

A crack of twigs. White frame.
Suddenly the tent collapses in and he is being hit with something.

Martin screams.

Blows raining down on him. He is knocked unconscious. Black.

EXT. FOREST - MORNING - DAY 4.

Gloaming light.

The tents are strewn about and shredded. Martin wakes wrapped in tent material.

He rubs his head. He gets up and hobbles about. He finds Alma in her tent. She is still unconscious. He finds a water bottle and drinks a bit. He tries to wake her. She comes too with a start. Then tries to get up.

MARTIN
Stay still…

He gives her a sip of water. Struggles to sit up. She rolls onto her knees and staggers up. She looks at the mud around the camp. Nothing.

She looks around. Martin stands up.

ALMA
What have we got left?

The two of them organize their belongings. Most of their stuff is gone.
Martin pulls the soil-testing-kit bag to him. He looks inside…

The soil-testing kit has gone.

Martin scrabbles about. His feet wet on the morning dew. He looks around for his shoes… he finds a pile of rocks with the radio and mobile phones smashed on it. Martin wipes his brow.

MARTIN
My shoes.

ALMA
They are gone? Mine too.

MARTIN
How are far are we from Doctor Wendle's camp?

ALMA
Half a day.

MARTIN
We have to warn her.

PART 2

THE MAN IN THE WOODS

EXT. FOREST - DAY 4.

Feet on path. In mud. On twigs. Martin struggles through the woods. Alma is lighter on her feet, she finds a way through. Thinking rather than trudging.

ALMA
Walk over here, it's easier.

MARTIN
Why would they steal our shoes?

ALMA
We were lucky that's all they did.

MARTIN
Taunting us, smashing the radio. Do you think it was the family from the tent that attacked us?

ALMA
I don't know.

They walk on.

Time passes. They walk up a hill, past a downed tree. It's quiet. Slow going.

Martin treads on something.

MARTIN
Oh shit… fuck…

He hops about in agony.

ALMA
What have you done?

MARTIN
Something sharp. A stone. Oh. Fuck it's bleeding.

He hops about.

EXT. FOREST - DAY 4.

Martin is sitting down. Alma washes his foot with water and tears off a bit of clothing and binds the foot.

She looks in the woods and comes back with a branch. She wraps more clothing around it to make a soft pad for his arm pit. She has made a crutch.

MARTIN
Thank you. I'm sorry.

ALMA
Just an accident.

MARTIN
You have an image of yourself in a crisis, this isn't it.

ALMA
It's fine, just calm down.

Alma looks at Martin. He is miserable. She starts up a conversation to distract him.

ALMA (CONT'D)
What was happening last night? With the lights by Doctor Wendle's camp?

MARTIN
I've been thinking about it. It's got no connection to her documented methods… She was conducting tests based around electrical impulses and hormones…

ALMA
To attempt to get a response out of the Mycorrhiza?

MARTIN
Yes. Plants can sense light and sound as well. They know when it's night…They react to the sound of caterpillars eating. They can emit chemicals to repel them.

She could be using that as an alternate way to communicate.

ALMA
What is she like, Doctor Wendle?

MARTIN
She didn't talk to me much at first. She didn't talk to many people. They sort of pushed her out. Her ideas were too radical for the Fashdale Institute. They are good people… but conservative at heart.
She came out here to get away from everyone I think.

ALMA
I can understand that.

MARTIN
I think you and Doctor Wendle are more in agreement than you think.

ALMA
I don't see nature the same way as you and Doctor Wendle seem to… as a puzzle to be solved and exploited. The more time I spend here, the more I feel I'm joining it.

EXT. FOREST - DAY 4.

Martin hobbles along. Alma just ahead. She stops.

Alma is aware of something moving in the woods. They stand still just listening. It's very quiet. Someone is there.

ALMA
HELLO.

Nothing.

They walk on unnerved.

ALMA (CONT'D)
Someone is watching us.

Martin throws a 'How can you tell?' look.

ALMA (CONT'D)
Listen…

They stand still panting for a moment.

ALMA (CONT'D)
There are no animals.

MARTIN
Why are they so quiet?

ALMA
Because they can sense something.

They walk on. Ahead they see a clearing. There is a man sitting there on the grass.

He stands up as they approach. A man in his 40s.

ZAC
Hello, travelers.

ALMA
Hello.

A slight pause

MARTIN
Someone stole our shoes.

ZAC
I can see that.

ALMA
What are you doing out here?

A pause as Zac looks at them

ZAC
I saw you two stumbling about and I thought. I should help them. But then I thought…

You are a park ranger and you probably don't want me living out here.

Alma smiles.

Pause.

MARTIN
But here you are.

Pause.

ZAC
I couldn't in good conscious let you limp around on your own. You could get hurt.

ALMA
I won't tell if you won't.

ZAC
That's very kind of you.

MARTIN
What is your name?

ZAC
Zac.

MARTIN
Martin and Alma.

ZAC
I presume you came through quarantine at the Gantalow lodge?

MARTIN
Yes.

ZAC
Still. Lets keep our distance. eh?

ALMA
Yes.

ZAC
I hope I didn't spook you.

MARTIN
No. Well a little bit.

ZAC
You can't be too careful.

He pulls up his arm and shows them a roughly bandaged cut.

ZAC (CONT'D)
Man and a Woman. Attacked me yesterday.

ALMA
Did they have a child?

ZAC
I didn't see one.

ALMA
We found an abandoned camp. There were kids' toys.

ZAC
Maybe they moved on.

Zac pulls his sleeve down and looks at their muddy feet.

ZAC (CONT'D)
I've got some shoes… If you want them. I think they will fit.

Martin looks to Alma.

She nods.

EXT. FOREST - DAY 4.

The three walk through the woods. Alma is cautious.

MARTIN
How long have you been out here?

ZAC
Long time now, before the pandemic.

EXT. ZAC'S TENT - DAY 4.

Zac takes them back to his tent. It's a rough, sprawling-looking place. Made from tarps and rope.

ZAC
Here we are.

Martin looks over to a second structure.

MARTIN
What is that?

ZAC
It's my workshop.

They duck down into the house.

They find themselves in a tarp vestibule.

ZAC (CONT'D)
Wait here.

Alma and Martin wait for a moment. Zac returns with a spray. He washes them down with disinfectant.

INT. ZAC'S TENT - DAY 4.

Alma and Martin move to one side of the tent.

MARTIN
Do you go to the town?

ZAC
For supplies… Once every couple of months. I like it less every time.

I assume you are here to visit Doctor Wendle.

Alma and Martin look at each other.

MARTIN
You know her?

Zac nods.

ZAC
I keep away out of respect for her work.

Zac looks at Martin's feet.

ZAC (CONT'D)
That is nasty… I think I need to wash and stitch it.

MARTIN
Stitch?

ZAC
Yes. It's flapping about. Come here.

Martin looks to Alma. What can he do? Zac washes his feet and then pulls out a little sewing kit.

ZAC (CONT'D)
Don't worry, I've done this before… I mean… On myself… Always getting caught on things.

Martin is in agony as Zac stitches up the deep scratch on his foot.

ZAC (CONT'D)
There you go. Good as new. FOOD!

Zac claps then leaves the room to prepare lunch. Martin looks around the room. It's quite packed with salvaged nicknacks, wood and reeds.

Time passes.

Zac comes back in smiling.

ZAC (CONT'D)
I haven't got much. Mostly foraged.

He cooks them food.

The three eat. Small talk. The food is nice. Zac pours some home-made cordial.

He puts down a pair of shoes and holds them up to Martin's feet. The right size.

ZAC (CONT'D)
It must have been hard going without shoes.

MARTIN
Thank you.

ALMA
How many more people have you seen out there?

ZAC
When I saw one family… I thought… Many will come, because people think as a herd.

There is one idea… And they all have it.

It's what makes people so easy to manipulate.

Zac picks up a guitar.

ZAC (CONT'D)
Listen to this.

He strums. The sounds are rich and resonating

ALMA
I don't feel right.

He strums again.

ZAC
Reassuring words… Or being kind. It triggers a social response. A trade of trust.

Again with a chord change.

ALMA
What have you done?

Alma slips under the table

ZAC
You must be sleepy. You need some rest

Martin's vision blurs. He sees Zac has stood up. Martin tries to stand but staggers to his feet. The world is on its side.

Zac picks at his guitar for a bit and steps out of Martin's field of view.

Martin sees something out of the corner of his eye. He hears Alma struggling. What is happening? It's deeply unsettling. Sobbing. crying.

Black.

He comes too and Zac is close to him. Taking Martin's clothes off.

ZAC (CONT'D)
Shhh Shhh it's fine. Shhhh.

INT. ZAC'S HUT - NIGHT - DAY 4.

Macro extreme-close-up shots: details of a 35mm-stills camera, film being processed. Flash bulbs going off.

A scalpel on skin. The peeling back of flesh. Then material dropped in, Flesh stitched up.

Shot from above:

A cut-out standing stone. Alma and Martin slumped on it like Adam and Eve.

Zac dressed with horns made of wood. Standing between them.

EXT. FOREST - MORNING - DAY 5.

The red sunlight peeks through the trees. Mist in the forest.

INT. ZAC'S HUT - MORNING - DAY 5.

Light just penetrates through the shuttered windows. Alma opens her eyes groggily. She looks across the room and sees Zac drinking a steaming-hot coffee. He's cutting up a piece of tarpaulin with a fret-saw blade. She tries to stand and finds that she is tied to the chair she is sitting in.

ALMA
What is this?

Martin wakes hearing the voices. He looks around alarmed.

ZAC
I'm sorry. I couldn't be sure how you would react.

MARTIN
Why are we tied up?

ZAC
You see.
You are agitated. Dangerous to me and dangerous to yourself.

ALMA
Let us go.

ZAC
I can't yet.

Look.

This is interesting.
Have you ever developed film.
It's fascinating.

Zac leaves the room.

MARTIN
Alma. My arm, I think he has done something to it.

Alma looks over and Martin shows her his arm. It's bandaged. Martin pulls at the bandage and it reveals a red mess of stitching and cuts.

MARTIN (CONT'D)
What is that?

ALMA
I don't know…

Zac returns and blacks out the windows and turns on a red light.

ZAC
Photography is like magic really.

But all technology is when you don't understand it.

Zac shows them pictures of them posed around the shack.

Obviously drugged. Him moving their mouths. He has a film developing kit. He processes the pictures as he talks to them.

He shows them pictures. Alma stares at the white paper as it slowly comes into focus.

Her and Martin. Dressed in home-made costumes. Posed in the studio. They come too, groggy.

ALMA
What are those clothes?

ZAC
You should relax. I'm not hurting you.

ALMA
Please let us go.

ZAC
I would but I can't now. It's not possible. Oh what do we have here?

He looks at where the bandage has come off Martin's arm

ZAC (CONT'D)
It will get infected

Zac sets about putting the bandage back on.

ZAC (CONT'D)
You don't want to get sepsis out here. You could die from that.

MARTIN
What is this?

ZAC
I'm marking you, Martin. So that he can see you. It's alright, I have them too.

He pulls up his shirt to display a series of scars.

ZAC (CONT'D)
Don't you feel him now? In the earth?

MARTIN
No. I don't know what you mean.

ZAC
I think you do.

Zac forces them to take more tranquilizers. It's harrowing. He grabs their faces and holds their noses forcing them to gasp out.

He pops the pills in their mouths and starts massaging their throats. Like you do when you are forcing a cat to take medicine.

Black

Amateur surgery. Stitching. Camera flashes.

INT. ZAC'S HUT - DAY 6.

They wake up and he shows them pictures of themselves again.

The pictures show the horned man holding the heads of Alma and Martin. It's as if he is relaying information to them.
Through his eyes.

White wood placed like lightning is arcing out of his eyes.

Another shows a man (Zac) plucking Martin's eyes out. Alma is seen collapsed on the floor.

ZAC
How are you faring?

MARTIN
What?

Martin looks at his arm. More bandages.

ZAC
How are you faring? You good? Settling in?

ALMA
Zac, please.

ZAC
Don't try and bargain with me. I can't let you see her.

ALMA
Doctor Wendle?

ZAC
Yes, Wendle.

ALMA
Why?

ZAC
I trusted her but she has profoundly misunderstood him. He has come to me and I talked to him. He's not interested in what she is offering. She wants to enslave him.

ZAC (CONT'D)
But he doesn't care.

JENNY
Who dosn't care?

ZAC (CONT'D)
She thinks that science appeals to him, but he's not interested. He likes Art. He likes flattery, sacrifice.

JENNY (CONT'D)
Who, Zac?

ZAC (CONT'D)
The thing in the woods. You know, Martin... She must have said... She thinks she can talk to him and bargain with him. I'm talking to him in a purer way. Making images. Praising him. Worshipping him. Did she not talk about it?

MARTIN
We haven't heard from her in months, Zac.

ZAC
I want to believe you Martin.

But people are essentially the same. They bargain with what they have. It doesn't take long till they get down to it. To become desperate. And say anything.

Believe me. He has sent me so many people in the last few months.

I suppose they were fleeing from the disease in the city. But they find their way to me. Drawn here. I bet you wished you had got your parents out of the city, Martin.

MARTIN
How do you know about that?

ZAC
In your diary.

Zac pulls out Martin's diary and flips through it.

ZAC (CONT'D)
Lots of good passages in here. Very candid. Lots of Boo-Hoo stuff about your elderly mother and father. Sorry to hear that. Bit of bad luck there. Chose the wrong branch of science to help them...

MARTIN
Yes.

ZAC
That is horrible. And you infected them? You must feel guilty.

Turning to Alma

ZAC (CONT'D)
He basically killed them. And you were fine. Asymptomatic. Did you catch it off a girl-friend, Martin? Someone you were knocking about with. Maybe at the lab?

Did you know this Alma?

ALMA
No.

ZAC
He's not the chatty type? No campfire confes-sions? Fair enough. Killed his own parents. I always thought the virus was a hoax. Maybe you brought something back from the lab that you worked at?

Zac peeks into the diary

ZAC (CONT'D)
"Doctor Wendle is one of the greatest scien-tific minds of her generation."
…And you had sex with her at Harringdon. You don't mention it in your diary… Maybe you were being coy…

MARTIN
No.

ZAC
Oh. Well that's unusual for her.

ALMA
Stop it.

ZAC
Oh I'm sorry, I thought he could talk for himself.

Zac turns and looks at Alma. He narrows his eyes.

ZAC (CONT'D)
What are you doing here?

ALMA
My job.

ZAC
Oh forgot. You are managing the forest for its own good. It doesn't need you. It knows what it wants. I've seen it.

ALMA
Seen what?

ZAC
Seen IT. I've seen inside the world.

You were drawn here to live in the land.

Did you ever consider what the ultimate expression of that was?

When you are completely separated from the process of humans.

When you return to the green, to its rhythms, rather than the selfish beat of humans.

I'm making flesh, what you know is right.

He puts the soil analyzer on the desk. They look at it for a moment.

ALMA
You attacked us in our tents.

ZAC
It wasn't an attack, it was a test.

ALMA
A test of what?

ZAC
Loyalty.
Anybody with any sense would have left. Run back to the lodge. But not you.

ALMA
YOU took our shoes!

ZAC
Yes, to make it harder to go forward.

MARTIN
But you gave us no choice but to go on.

ZAC
I'm not stupid, Martin. I can't be won over. You are approaching this all wrong. This isn't your world anymore. It's MINE.

Zac bangs the table.

ZAC (CONT'D)
Your world is shrunk. Your world is sleeping and ritual. Praising him.

ALMA
Who?

ZAC
Parnag Fegg.

Theres is a silence… Zac looks at Alma. He smiles.

ZAC (CONT'D)
You know that name?

ALMA
Yes.

ZAC
I would expect a park ranger to recognize it.

Zac gets some photographs. They have other drugged people in them.

ZAC (CONT'D)
He told me his story. He was persecuted and hunted through these woods. They said he was a practicing necromancer and alchemist.

You know how people can be.
Intolerant.

All they found was an ancient standing stone. He had gone.

Inducted into the stone. Transferred into the ancient matter of the forest.

Zac shows them pictures showing Fegg-costumed victims posing lanterns around the fake standing stone

ZAC (CONT'D)
Over the millennia people reported sightings of him. A stranger was said to help people who were lost. But he wasn't trying to help. He was asking for help. He was trapped here.

MARTIN
Do you believe that?

ZAC
I believe I can hear him coursing in my ears.
I honor him with images. These are his memories.

Martin and Alma look at Zac in mute terror

ZAC (CONT'D)
I'm sorry I lost my temper.

His shirt is undone, and for the first time we can see his neck. There is a slash mark across it.

Zac sees Martin looking.

ZAC (CONT'D)
I told you I was always catching myself on things.

Zac ignores them. He goes back to making costumes for the next night's photo shoot.

Cut to Black

Zac is stitching together tarps. He cuts through them with a length of fret-saw. He looks over as he senses someone outside. He gets up and the fret-saw blade drops to the floor.

Zac walks over to the door and goes outside. Martin can hear him talking to someone. Alma is passed out. Martin comes too.

Voices are raised. The high-pitched murmur of argument, a slap. Then Zac comes back inside rubbing his face.

He pulls out a packet of pills. He counts them and frowns. He grinds up two in a pestle and mortar.

Martin watches him out of the corner of his eye. Zac comes over with a glass of water for Martin to drink.

ZAC (CONT'D)
Don't fight me, Martin.

Black.

INT. ZAC'S HUT - DAY 7.

Martin comes too. He is groggy. His POV is blurred. He looks over to Alma. Zac is not in the hut. More bandages are on his body now.

MARTIN
Alma.

Alma slowly opens her eyes.

MARTIN (CONT'D)
He's going to kill us.

ALMA
I think so.

He looks around the shack slowly. There's nothing there. Alma spots the bit of fret-saw on the floor.

MARTIN
He has given us a smaller dose.

ALMA
Must be running out. Play along with him.

MARTIN
Ok.

ALMA
I can get to that… (she eyes the fret blade on the floor) and cut through… Then I'll hit him with something and then we run in opposite directions.

MARTIN
Why?

ALMA
I'll lead him away, you are too slow.

MARTIN
What if he chases me?

ALMA
If I hit him, he will chase me… Walk towards the sun and you will end up at Doctor Wendle's camp.
I'll find you there.

MARTIN
I heard him talking to someone.

Alma thinks.

ALMA
Ok. I'll keep an eye open.

Zac enters the tent. He sniffs the air. He moves over to Martin's foot and unbandages it.

ZAC
Oh.

He turns and looks at Martin

ZAC (CONT'D)
We have bad situation. I think that your foot is infected. We have two courses of action. I could get you too a hospital. But I think it would take too long. We are 30 miles from any civilization and could take days.

MARTIN
What is the alternative?

ZAC
Amputation. I mean, not the whole foot. Just some toes.

MARTIN
Just some toes

ZAC
Yes. I'm really sorry. But my axe is pretty sharp. You shouldn't feel it.

MARTIN
Axe?

Zac pulls out his axe. He moves a log over.

ZAC
Pop your foot on there.

Martin struggles.

MARTIN
Oh no… get me to the hospital.

ZAC
If you struggle it's only going to make it much worse

ALMA
Take him to the hospital.

ZAC
I explained. There is no time. This is for the best. Now hold still.

Zac grabs Martin's foot and swings. Martin screams. Zac looks down and frowns. The little toe is gone, but the tow next to it is flapping about.

ZAC (CONT'D)
It's half off. I told you to be still.

He swings again and severs the other toe.

ZAC (CONT'D)
There. I know it feels harsh. But that was life and death.

INT. ZAC'S HUT - NIGHT - DAY 7.

Close-up sewing.

Twine being cut, Twigs being cut. Photographs of bodies.

ZAC
(SINGING)
Now is come September, the hunters moon begun, And through the wheaten stubble is heard the frequent gun. The leaves are pale and yellow, and kindling into red,
All among the barley, who would not be blithe?

When the ripe and bearded barley is smiling on the scythe.
And the ripe and bearded barley is hanging down its head.
The spring is like a young man who does not know his mind. The summer is a tyrant of most ungracious kind. The autumn's like an

old friend, who loves one all she can, And she brings the bearded barley to glad the heart of man.

He finishes off Martin's costume.

INT. ZAC'S HUT - DAY 8.

Zac drags Martin through the house to where his wooden studio is. He leaves Martin there on the floor. His foot in a large bandage.

Zac goes back to his hut. He looks around. Where is Alma?

ALMA
Arrrrrrgh.

She smashes him with the photo enlarger. It comes on as she is hitting him, making light bounce around the room.

Martin collapses to the floor. Blood pouring from his head.

Alma moves outside. To free Martin. She looks around wildly, where is he?

MARTIN
Help… Over here.

Alma runs.

She gets to Martin and starts cutting at his bind-ings.

MARTIN (CONT'D)
What happened?

ALMA
I hit him as hard as I could.

MARTIN
Did you kill him?

ALMA
I hope so.

At that moment they hear movement. Alma ducks out and sees Zac coming out of his hut. She runs back to Martin

ALMA (CONT'D)
Come on...

She looks back and can see Zac dragging an axe.

MARTIN
Oh please.

Alma looks out again and sees Zac slowly moving forward

MARTIN (CONT'D)
Don't leave me, please.

Alma manages to cut through the last of Martin's bindings. He gets up woozie.

MARTIN (CONT'D)
Oh...

ALMA
He's coming.

Zac enters the small hut. Blood running down his face. The wound on his head looks bad. A glint of white bone sticking through the blood.

ZAC
Get back in the house!

Zac raises the axe.

MARTIN
Put it down, Zac!

ZAC
Get back in the house, I don't want to hurt you.

He swings the axe. But he is too badly hurt to make a connection.

ALMA
RUN!

Martin runs. He looks back and Alma is throwing things in Zac's way. He is batting them away with the axe.

She hits him with a chair and he falls back and she runs as well.

MARTIN
Run, Alma. Run...

Martin is looking towards the hut as he speaks. He trips and falls backwards.

Martin falls and rolls. He has fallen into a shallow grave. The corpses of the missing campers are there. They have been butchered.

He falls into their bodies. Guts split, maggots, grue. Blood on his face. He gasps in shock. Martin makes a mess of getting out of the pit. It's slippery and difficult.

His hand goes into a chest cavity. A corpse gasps, pushing spores into the air like a puffball.

Zac runs back into the house and then appears with a compound bow.

Martin gets up trying to rub the blood off his face. He looks back and sees Zac appearing.

MARTIN (CONT'D)
Oh god, he's got a bow... ALMA!!

Zac fires an arrow. It thrrrps through the air and into a tree. Alma runs in zig zags.

Martin runs in the opposite direction. He looks back and sees that Zac has taken after Alma.

MARTIN (CONT'D)
OVER HERE!! OVER HERE!

He watches as Zac fires at Alma. Sees her fall in the distance.

MARTIN (CONT'D)
NO...

Zac turns and fires another arrow at Martin. An arrow hits a tree.

Martin shrieks. He turns and runs into the woods. He runs and gasps, looking back and seeing Zac chasing him.

He looks back after a while and Zac is no longer there. He sits down and gasps for air.

He looks for the sun and sets off in that direction.

The light starts to go. He makes a shelter out of leaves and grass and curls up in it.

EXT. FOREST - EVENING - DAY 8.

Martin wakes. He takes in the sound of the woods. Wind blowing. He looks at some insects going about their business. Takes in the bird song. He gets up and stretches. Aching.

He is really thirsty and finds a puddle and drinks from it.

He looks at mushrooms but is too afraid to try them. He keeps limping along on his bad foot. Looking at the sun.

He sits down and sobs.

MARTIN
Alma.

Alma is dead. It's his fault.

PART 3

DOCTOR WENDLE

EXT. FOREST - EVENING - DAY 8.

The light is fading. Martin Stumbles through the woods. Looking around, wary of Zac. That he is out there somewhere… Stalking him.

Mist.

Martin is hobbling on his foot. He sits down and looks at the bandage. He is scared to look at the wound.

He looks at his arms, covered in bandages. He pulls them off and sees three stitched-up wounds.

MARTIN
Oh. What is this?

He touches the wounds but recoils in agony. He sees a figure up ahead, faint in the mist.

MARTIN (CONT'D)
Hello?

The figure moves off. Moving between trees in the distance. Martin hobbles after them. He can't keep up. He walks on. He gets to a bit of open ground. He looks across to another valley. He can see a man. He smiles and goes to wave, then stops. It's Zac. Oh god.

He watches the small figure moving relentlessly forward carrying an axe.

Zac looks over and sees him. Tiny in the distance, he moves behind some trees and disappears.

There is a noise in the woods. A long bass note. It echoes around. Martin turns towards it and starts to move.

MARTIN (CONT'D)
No. No...

Martin hobbles back into the woods. He is hyperventilating, trying to push himself forward. Terrified. He trips and falls and rolls into the undergrowth.

He sees an electrical wire on the floor. He pulls it and sees that more of it is hidden under leaves. He moves along pulling at the wire until he gets to a wooden box. It has a microphone in it.

He speaks into it...

MARTIN (CONT'D)
Hello, is anyone there?

He waits, feeling a little foolish. He looks around. Is anyone watching? Nothing... He walks on ...

He finds another microphone...

MARTIN (CONT'D)
Hello?

He looks around. Then there is squark and feedback... Obviously coming from some kind of speaker set up. A voice echoes through the woods.

SPEAKER (A WOMANS VOICE)
Hello?

MARTIN
Help me, please...

EXT. FOREST - EVENING - DAY 8.

Zac stops in his tracks. He has heard the voice too. He is pale from blood loss. Head bandaged roughly. Blood down face. He re-doubles his efforts.

ZAC
MARTIN!

EXT. FOREST - EVENING - DAY 8.

Martin hears Zac's voice in the distance. He cowers away from him. The sun is setting. He hides deeper away from the path.

MARTIN
Oh god, oh god. Please let me get through this.

He watches Zac get closer.

ZAC
I know you are there. You are so easy to track… Lumbering about. Gulump gulump.

Martin watches with alarm as he gets closer and closer.

We see the axe head, shining, cutting through the bracken like an inverted sharks fin.

A deep rumble starts. Quiet at first then louder and louder.

Zac puts his hands over his ears.

Then it rises to almost deafening proportions. It's hard to tell where it's coming from. The woodland acts like amphitheater. Zac rubs his bandaged head as the sound agitates him.

EXT. FOREST - NIGHT - DAY 8.

Martin takes this opportunity to crawl away. Through the bracken and undergrowth. Like a worm. He crawls towards the sound.

It's very blue and dark now. Suddenly there is a flash of white. Martin shields his eyes.
Lights light up the place and there is the sound of loud, deep rumbles. Strobe lights and sound waves.

EXT. FOREST - NIGHT - DAY 8.

Zac can see Martin as he is lit up by the strobes.

A silhouette. Against the trees. Then multiple shadows. There is silence.
Then a deep resonating…

Boooooooooooooom. Followed by the clatter of strobes all over the area.

Zac shields his eyes as he stalks Martin. He's lost him again now. He slashes at the bracken with his axe.

The light is starting to burn his eyes. Traces melting onto his retina like an old tube tv. Zac rubs harder. He can't make him out.

EXT. FOREST - NIGHT - DAY 8.

Martin panics, he crawls faster. At the floor level it's like a series of fireworks going off over head. The sound is oppressive. A deep pulsing bass with a shrill climbing screech.

Martin thinks he is going to be killed. He can hear Zac calling in the woods. Looking for him.

EXT. FOREST - NIGHT - DAY 8.

Zac finds a light and kicks it over. It starts firing up into the branches. He fumbles in his pocket and pulls out a flare. He rips the top off it and it ignites. He lights up the forest with it… It bubbles blood red, his face demonic.

The strobe starts going quicker with the tempo of the music. It's like a machine gun now. Blasting all around Zac.

Zac holds his head. Blood is running down his forehead from where Alma hit him.

ZAC
Arhhhh…

He sees a figure in the strobes. Shadows. Everything is slow. The sound drops out.

White flash from another direction… Like the sun rising… The figure from before. Mist.
Zac panics.

ZAC (CONT'D)
What do you want me to do?

No answer. Zac stumbles back.

Then his face contorts. As if he has heard something we have missed.

ZAC (CONT'D)
I'm sorry… I'm sorry

He backs away.
The music is screaming white noise. A woodpecker of screaming synth. Every step forward Zac takes, it becomes more intense like a Geiger counter over a radioactive rock.

Zac turns and runs.

As he leaves, the pace of the strobes dies down. The music calms.

EXT. FOREST - NIGHT - DAY 8.

Martin crawls…

The music steadies. He gets deeper into the trees. Ahead he sees a figure moving between the trunks in the distance. Not Zac… Someone.

Martin finds himself in a clearing near a large standing stone.

He recognizes it from Zac's photographs.

The stone is nine feet tall and cold to touch. There is a hole in the middle of it. Martin reaches towards it.

He sees that on the stone there are marks that match the scars on his arms.

He backs away from the stone with fear.

He bumps into someone, a figure in full hazmat equipment…

He looks up, terrified.

The figure pulls him up and helps him walk. Moves him through the braken and strobe flashes.

The figure gives him some water. Martin drinks thankfully.

FIGURE
Come on.

They move off. Martin is in a bewildered state of shock.

EXT. FOREST - NIGHT - DAY 8.

Zac staggers along.

We see his POV. The strobe has burnt his retinas He rubs his eyes… trying to see.
He collapses against a tree.

The bass noise starts again in the woods. Zac holds his hands to his head.

He pulls at moss from a tree and tucks it into the wound in his head. He pushes it in with his fingers and slides down the side of the tree and passes out.

Macro root detail. Close up of the mycorrhiza. Sparking under the soil.

We see his POV. The flickering lights still sparking in his mind.

EXT. FOREST - EVENING - DAY 8.

Close-up hand-washing. Martin is scrubbing himself clean. The figure stands back from him. She throws him a virus test stick in a fresh sealed box.

FIGURE
Use it.

He unwraps it and swabs his tongue. The figure looks at him, assessing him.
He shows her the negative swab. He is clean of infection. She takes off her respirator.

DOCTOR OLIVIA WENDLE.

A flash of light illuminates her. Martin blinks in terror, then she smiles, recognizing him.

DOCTOR WENDLE
Martin?

Martin shouts. His hearing has been effected by the loud noises.

MARTIN
IS THAT YOU?

Doctor Wendle puts her finger to her mouth… shhh…

DOCTOR WENDLE
What are you doing here, Martin? What are these?

Doctor Wendle grabs his arm looking at the scars. Martin pulls away, wild eyed.

DOCTOR WENDLE (CONT'D)
What happened to your foot?

MARTIN
He cut my toes off…

Wendle looks nervously at Martin.

DOCTOR WENDLE
Come with me, I need to get you back to the camp.

EXT. WENDLE'S CAMP - NIGHT - DAY 8.

Martin and Doctor Wendle approach the campsite. It's hidden in the woods. Secret.

Three tents with sheltered tarps.

MARTIN
Is Alma here? She said she would meet me here.

Two of the tents are open. One is zipped up. A fire. Clothes drying. A generator. Solar Panels.

Wendle gets out of her Hazmat suit. Underneath… practical woodland gear. She gestures to one of the tents.

DOCTOR WENDLE
Stay here. I'll see if I can find her.

She grabs some bedding from her tent and brings it over, drops it down. Martin collapses.

MARTIN
I'm coming with you.

He scrambles to his feet.

DOCTOR WENDLE
You are in no fit state.

MARTIN
I have to come with you.

Doctor Wendle nods. Okay.

Wendle walks over to her tent. She quickly changes the settings on a complicated control panel. She pulls down the sound to a low hum and then turns the lights up.

The two of them walk into the woods.

MARTIN (CONT'D)
What have you been doing out here?

They walk through the flashing arrays of light.

MARTIN (CONT'D)
This is amazing.

She stops for a moment

DOCTOR WENDLE
Stay here. I can see something. Make sure she doesn't double back round and get past us.

Martin watches the doctor disappear into the undergrowth. He looks at the lights, marveling at the complexity. He looks at his hands, observing the dancing patterns.

There is an eerie noise. Loud, deep, throbbing bass. High-frequency modulating tones.

The forest is lit up by strobes. Some fast, some slower. Martin walks on a bit, lost in the light and the haunting sound bath.

Then he comes back across the large standing stone deep.

He looks at it's cold, wet face glinting in the moonlight. The music builds to a crescendo

Then silence, just Martin's breath.

Then he hears a noise. A scrabbling in the under-growth. He picks up a branch, gets ready to defend himself.
He sees a figure in the bracken.

As he raises the branch to hit the figure. A strobe light lights up…

A bloodied face…

Alma!

EXT. WENDLE'S CAMP - NIGHT 8.

Martin crashes into the camp pulling Alma along.

MARTIN
HELP!

Doctor Wendle runs in from the woods and looks over in alarm. She runs off into a tent and comes back with a medicine box. She gives Alma a tongue virus test…

Martin is sweating and starts to feel the world turning around him. He collapses down.

Alma and Doctor Wendle stare at each other for a moment. The sound of the array comes to a halt.
Martin looks up to Alma

MARTIN (CONT'D)
I thought you had died…

She struggles to smile.

EXT. WENDLE'S CAMP - MORNING - DAY 9.

Sunrise. Low-laying fog.

Doctor Wendle looks at Martin and Alma. She looks worried.

DOCTOR WENDLE
You will have to forgive me, I haven't talk-ed to anyone in months.

She smiles. Then looks seriously at them.

DOCTOR WENDLE (CONT'D)
I'm so sorry about what happened to you both.

Doctor Wendle looks at Martin's foot.

DOCTOR WENDLE (CONT'D)
There was no way of warning you about how dangerous the situation had become with Zac.

MARTIN
He's killed people. I saw bodies out there.

Doctor Wendle looks confused for a moment.

DOCTOR WENDLE
Killed?

ALMA
At least one family maybe more.

Doctor Wendle sits down, broken. She looks at Mar-tin's foot.

DOCTOR WENDLE
May I?

She starts to unwrap his bandage.

MARTIN
Who is he?

Doctor Wendle looks worried. Awkward.

DOCTOR WENDLE
Zac is my ex-husband.

They look confused.

DOCTOR WENDLE (CONT'D)
It's a very complicated situation.

She sees his mutilated toes. Alma looks. She can't help herself.

DOCTOR WENDLE (CONT'D)
Oh Martin…

She stops and composes herself.

DOCTOR WENDLE (CONT'D)
I'm sorry, this is all very upsetting.

She looks at his foot and frowns.

DOCTOR WENDLE (CONT'D)
This needs cauterizing.

ALMA
At a hospital?

DOCTOR WENDLE
There is no time for that.

She walks away to get some equipment. They sit there for a moment. Martin rubs his face and looks at Alma.

MARTIN
I'm sorry I left you back there. I don't know what to say…

Alma brushes it off.

ALMA
That was the plan. We said I would run and find you. It's fine.

She looks over to Wendle.

ALMA (CONT'D)
Something is very wrong here… What happened between them?

MARTIN
I don't know.

ALMA
I saw something in the woods last night… Did you?

Doctor Wendle looks over to the two of them speaking. She can see their lips moving but can't hear them.
Doctor Wendle walks over with her medical kit bag.

DOCTOR WENDLE
I didn't think anyone was coming.

She sets up her equipment. Wendle puts a metal implement in the fire.

MARTIN
When your letters stopped I just assumed you wanted some space.

DOCTOR WENDLE
I could't talk to you any more. I couldn't talk to anyone. My initial line of experimentation failed. Months and months of dead ends.

Martin looks at what Wendle is preparing…

MARTIN
What are you going to do?

DOCTOR WENDLE
I'm sorry Martin. I'm going to have cauterize that wound or it is going to get infected.

MARTIN
You are going to burn me?

DOCTOR WENDLE
Yes. Alma can you hold him for me…

Alma nods mutely. She grabs hold of him…

MARTIN
Aren't I supposed to bite on something?

Doctor Wendle smiles and passes him a piece of wood. She turns to her work…
Doctor Wendle presses the white hot metal onto Martin's foot. Martin screams loud then passes out.

EXT. WENDLE'S CAMP - DAY 9.

Time has passed. Martin's foot is now bandaged. He is still unconscious.

ALMA
How long till he can move?

DOCTOR WENDLE
I think a day or so.

She stops and looks at Alma concerned.

DOCTOR WENDLE (CONT'D)
How are you?

ALMA
I don't know yet.

DOCTOR WENDLE
I can't tell you how sorry I am.

ALMA
It's not your fault. You didn't attack us.

Martin comes round. He looks up at the two women.

MARTIN
I can't feel anything.

DOCTOR WENDLE
Don't worry it will wear off soon.
Then it will really sting. Martin smiles.

ALMA
You said that your research had stalled.

DOCTOR WENDLE
The Fashdale Institute wanted results. I had nothing.

I spent weeks walking on my own in the woods, sleeping outside. Just lost, and then I found the stone.I don't know how I had missed it.
But it had been there all along.
It was like it was calling to me.
I started to study it… I used it to take my mind off my own work. I thought I could shake myself out of the hole I was in.

Doctor Wendle smiles and goes back to her tent, talking as she goes…

DOCTOR WENDLE (CONT'D)
The markings on the stone led me down a rabbit hole of research before I found this book.

She returns with an old book in a tough plastic jacket.

DOCTOR WENDLE (CONT'D)
This contains amongst other things… an English translation of Malleus Maleficarum - the Hammer of the Witches. The book is dated 1640, but there has been multiple rebind-

ings. Some of the pages are much older and from other books.
There is a section in the back where this forest is mentioned.

She opens it to a page with an illustration on. It shows two figures standing by the standing stone surrounded by lanterns. It could be mistaken for a strange wedding ceremony.

ALMA
These images are similar to the images Zac showed us. He said it was Parnag Fegg.

DOCTOR WENDLE
Parnagg Fegg.

The name translates in the local dialect as "Sound," "PARNAGUS" and "light," "FEGG." Heart felt prayer and gods light. I don't think she was a person at all. I think it was a process.

Fegg is a composite character cobbled together over millenia. A lot of what Zac believes is ancient is only Victorian, Some of the Parnag Fegg legend was cooked up in the 70s.

They look at an illustration showing a ritual

DOCTOR WENDLE (CONT'D)
But it got me thinking, obviously they wouldn't have gotten anywhere with torches and drums.
But with modern equipment…

Maybe I could. So in the end what I was using to take my mind of my research… solved it. It's funny how you can being doing something and not even realize it. Zac came to the forest and he helped me set up this new experiment.

MARTIN
Why get Zac involved? Why not ask the board at the Fashdale Institute?

DOCTOR WENDLE
They would have never grasped this. It was all too important to risk.

Martin looks at the illustrations in the book.

MARTIN
So you are using light and sound to communicate?

DOCTOR WENDLE
YES. The lights pulse in reaction to the feedback the microphones give me from the trees.

ALMA
What feedback?

DOCTOR WENDLE
Plants can make noise, the trees can actually control a lot of the sounds the branches make. Even the roots make sounds at a certain frequency.

Martin nods. 20HZ apparently.

DOCTOR WENDLE (CONT'D)
Once you filter out the wind and the other woodland noises, there are definite patterns. Through these reactions I've created a very basic language.

Martin looks at the pattern forming on the monitor. It rolls around in fractal dance.

MARTIN
That can't be real.

DOCTOR WENDLE
It's real. There is something in there and it's talking back

MARTIN
Incredible.

DOCTOR WENDLE
But that was the problem… What it said to Zac.
We tried to make contact with the Mycorrhiza in a more direct way, according to the rites in the book.
We pushed it too far…

Well he was never the same again.
Whatever Zac saw terrified him. He ran. I didn't see him for months until I found him living in the opposite valley. He barely recognized me. He was wild.

ALMA
Why did you use the ritual in the book? That seems like a contradiction.

DOCTOR WENDLE
A contradiction of what?

ALMA
You. Your research here.

DOCTOR WENDLE
I'm reacting to the results. Using the book seemed to accelerate the progress. I had to learn to have an open mind. I'm surprised you don't. Time passes

Doctor Wendle watches from her tent as she prepares some food. She walks over.

ALMA
Thank you.

Doctor Wendle looks at the wounds on Martin's arm.

DOCTOR WENDLE
…I'm very concerned about these.

Martin looks at the swollen lumps on his arm.

DOCTOR WENDLE (CONT'D)
We need to open them up. I think there is something under the skin.

INT. DOCTOR WENDLE'S TENT - DAY 9.

Wendle sterilizes her equipment. Martin sits on a chair with his arm resting on a table. She starts to inject around the wounds.
She starts to dig into one of the scars with her scalpel. She struggles slightly.

DOCTOR WENDLE
It's tough. It's animal gut I think.

She opens the wound like a drawstring bag. Alma makes a face at the putrid smell.

ALMA
Oh.

Doctor Wendle looks inside and pokes around with her scalpel.

MARTIN
What is it?

Doctor Wendle picks some grey mushy particles out and drops them in a petri dish.

DOCTOR WENDLE
I don't know. But it looks organic.

Doctor Wendle finds a small silver charm in the flesh. She tweezers it out and drops it into a metal bowl with a TINK.

MARTIN
He put a charm under my skin?

DOCTOR WENDLE
I wouldn't try to understand it in logical terms.

The doctor gets up and goes towards her tent.

ALMA
Just tell me what you need. I can get it.

Alma goes to follow but Doctor Wendle steps out and blocks her way.

DOCTOR WENDLE
Please don't come in here. I'm trying to keep it sterile as I can.

ALMA
Ok.

She turns and zips the tent up.

MARTIN
The shapes of the scars match the markings on the stone.

DOCTOR WENDLE (OFF SCREEN)
Pattern-making. He's trying to make meaning where there isn't any.

Doctor Wendle returns with another bottle of sterilized water.

DOCTOR WENDLE (CONT'D)
It's a psychological problem with humans. We want to make stories out of everything.

She locks the tent. Alma watches her then looks at the computer and mixing-desk set-up that Wendle has under a sunshade near her tent.

DOCTOR WENDLE (CONT'D)
He thinks he can communicate with nature through art and worship.
It's idolatry. He isn't interested in a scientific path.

She opens up the last wound. She looks concerned. Under the skin is a mat of fungus.

She picks at it with tweezers. Martin pulls away.

DOCTOR WENDLE (CONT'D)
It's bonded with your flesh. That is very unusual.

Martin screams as the doctor pulls the fibrous tendrils of the fungus out of his arm. She swabs the wound down with alcohol. Martin screams more.

MARTIN
Oh god.

DOCTOR WENDLE
He's not here though, is he?

Martin tries to smile. But he can't

MARTIN
What is unusual?

DOCTOR WENDLE
That the infection would take hold so quickly. You have special flesh Martin.

This is not reassuring. Time passes.
Doctor Wendle is re-bandaging Martin's arm

She touches his arm, then takes his hand and leads him over to the control desk.

DOCTOR WENDLE (CONT'D)
Come and see.

She passes out headphones and then initiates the system. Lights flash in the forest and sound rises. The doctor demonstrates the system in action. Showing the trees responding to the sounds and light with sound of their own.

The computer shows a pulsing graphical representation of the forest responding to the sounds. She shows a graphic with a map. It shows the are. There seems to be a large pulsating blob showing on the screen.

DOCTOR WENDLE (CONT'D)
It all emanates from the standing stone. That is where there is the densest cluster of Mycorrhizae.

It regulates this forest for 30 square miles, but I think it might be bigger still.

ALMA
How big?

DOCTOR WENDLE
Country wide.

MARTIN
Really?

DOCTOR WENDLE
Where ever there is nature, wherever the roots reach and the Mycorrhizae can extend and connect.

Nature is one giant system and this is the key to communicate with it.

I'm so close to a real breakthrough. It makes sense that you are here to witness it.

She smiles at the thought.

ALMA
But we are not waiting that, are we? We are going as soon as Martin can move

DOCTOR WENDLE
You want to leave after I've shown you all of this?

ALMA
We don't have any choice. It's only a matter of time before Zac comes here looking for us. He can't let us live after what we have seen.

DOCTOR WENDLE
This is a mistake. Explain to her, we can't just walk away.

Wendle gets up and walks towards her tent.

ALMA
I don't trust her, Martin.

MARTIN
What do you mean?

ALMA
It's all too good to be true. Our escape from Zac. You said you heard another person. What if that was her?

MARTIN
She said she was being held prisoner here.

ALMA
He never came here in all that time? He was just over the hill. Wouldn't it make more sense if they were still working together?

MARTIN
Working at what?

ALMA
Did you know she was married?

MARTIN
No.

ALMA
She must have said something about herself.

MARTIN
When?

ALMA
When you had a relationship.

Theres a pause.

MARTIN
That's private.

ALMA
Yes, but under the circumstances it's relevant. What happened between them?

MARTIN
She didn't talk about other relationships. This is the first I've heard of a husband.

ALMA
You need to talk to her. Convince her.

MARTIN
There is no way she will leave this place.

He sits down dejected.

ALMA
This why you came here, isn't it, to see her?

MARTIN
I thought it was.

ALMA
If you care about her. You will get her to leave.

EXT. WOODS - DAY 9.

Martin watches Doctor Wendle from a distance. She is sobbing, sitting in the woods.
He approaches.

MARTIN
Olivia.

DOCTOR WENDLE
I'm sorry… I just. It shook me when I heard how bad Zac had gotten.

Wendle looks up and wipes her eyes, she assesses Martin. Reading him.

DOCTOR WENDLE (CONT'D)
You can't convince me to leave.
It's pointless now anyway...

MARTIN
What do you mean?

Doctor Wendle moves off and Martin follows.

DOCTOR WENDLE
I was drawn here. It was like I didn't have a choice.

They arrive at the standing stone.

DOCTOR WENDLE (CONT'D)
It's odd that the stone appears on no maps. The only mention of it I can find is in that book.

Doctor Wendle pulls out a trowel and starts digging at the foot of the stone.

DOCTOR WENDLE (CONT'D)
Why did you volunteer to come?

MARTIN
I wanted to see you. All the time I spent in lockdown, I thought about us.

DOCTOR WENDLE
Did the thought grow inside you like a seed?
A voice in your head you couldn't deny?

MARTIN
Maybe.

DOCTOR WENDLE
I felt the same way, when I came here. I lied before.
I got Zac involved, but I didn't call him.
He turned up like you did. He said the same thing. He couldn't deny the urge.
I found him here by the stone. The same way I found you... and you found Alma.

MARTIN
Are you saying I came here against my will?

DOCTOR WENDLE
You were drawn here too.

MARTIN
I wanted to come. To see you.

DOCTOR WENDLE
The Mycorrhizal network brings resources for the forest from many miles. Maybe it brought you.

MARTIN
How could that be possible?

DOCTOR WENDLE
Did you have ringworm?

MARTIN
Yes.

DOCTOR WENDLE
Zac and I had it too. I wonder what it was doing in our bodies. Pushing our body chemistry in certain directions. Like obsession, love?

Doctor Wendle pulls out a fibrous white material from the hole by the standing stone. She drops it into a Tupperware box.

DOCTOR WENDLE (CONT'D)
Think about why we are here. How important it is. This isn't chance. You can't fight it.

She smiles sadly.

PART 4

THE ESCAPE

EXT. WENDLE'S CAMP - MORNING - DAY 10.

Martin is shaken awake by Alma.

ALMA
The doctor is gone.

MARTIN
Are you sure?

ALMA
I can't find her.

MARTIN
Where would she go? She was adamant about not leaving. She couldn't have gone far. How long has it been light?

ALMA
Half an hour.

INT. FOREST - DAY 10.

Martin limps further into the woods. Alma follows reluctantly. We see puffball fungus gently emitting spores.

Alma stops.

ALMA
That's odd.

MARTIN
What?

ALMA
I've suddenly got a terrible headache.

Martin stops and shakes his head. A migraine squeezes his brain.

ALMA (CONT'D)
What is that… oh no…

Alma steps back in horror clutching her head in pain. Martin stops for a moment trying to take it in.

MARTIN
Alma, stop.

She starts to cough, stumbles on for a few feet.

Her breathing is getting heavy. Labored. Her feet seem heavy disrupting dust in the undergrowth. There seems to be a haze in the air.

Then she senses a person. He stops.

ALMA
Hello.

Alma wheels around she sees a shape. A shadow. Twigs crunch, but she can't hear it over her own breathing now.

ALMA (CONT'D)
Who is there?

Alma's breath quickens as she starts to become increasingly worried. A wave of heavy anxiety hits her. She is desperate for air.
No, worse, she is choking. She can't breathe, she's drowning…

Alma falls to her knees.

MARTIN
Oh god…

Martin grabs hold of Alma and pulls her back through the bracken. They collapse together for a moment, stunned.

Alma and Martin stagger back to the camp. Black.

EXT. WENDLE'S CAMP - MORNING - DAY 11.

Martin wakes with a start. He looks around. Early-morning orange light. Martin gets up holding his head and walks over to Alma.

Doctor Wendle approaches.

DOCTOR WENDLE
Anxiety, vision blurred?

ALMA
Yes.

MARTIN
Where did you go?

DOCTOR WENDLE
Extra acoustic and visual stimuli?

ALMA
Hallucination. Nausea yes.

DOCTOR WENDLE
I was checking the readings from monitoring devices out in the woods. I came back and you were both gone.

Alma is not so sure about her answer.
Time passes.
Alma watches as Doctor Wendle works on her computers. She turns to Martin.

ALMA
Everything seems to keep us here.

MARTIN
You suspect her?

ALMA
She has made contact with whatever is living under the forest. She said that herself.

MARTIN
Why would she want to keep us here?

EXT. EDGE OF WENDLE'S CAMP - DAY 11.

The three walk around the camp. Looking at the low mist. Alma marks it out on a map.

ALMA
The mist seems to start about half a mile out.

Doctor Wendle spots something.

MARTIN
What is it?

DOCTOR WENDLE
The forest is acting to contain us.

She bends down to pick a puffball mushroom.

ALMA
How is that possible?

DOCTOR WENDLE.
I've seen it before. With Zac. It forced him out of the valley.

She puts it in a bag and walks back to the camp. Alma is concerned.

ALMA
Why didn't you tell us that before?

DOCTOR WENDLE
Sorry, I didn't say? It's hard to keep track of all the information.

ALMA
No you didn't. Why would you hold that back?

Doctor Wendle holds her ground.

DOCTOR WENDLE
You blunder in here without knowing the first thing about the situation and I'm to blame?

Alma shifting gears.

ALMA
We use your hazmat suit and walk through it.

DOCTOR WENDLE
And what if the mist is less than 5 microns? It will go straight through the filters.

Alma hadn't thought of that.

ALMA.
It has to be worth a try.

DOCTOR WENDLE
We should wait it out. When it happened before, it only lasted a day or so.

She walks off. Martin and Alma watch her. Alma shakes her head in bemusement.

EXT. WENDLE'S CAMP - MORNING - DAY 11.

Martin looks over at Doctor Wendle in her tent. She is looking through data on her laptop and making notes.

ALMA
We just need to use her suit and push through it.

MARTIN
And then what? Run into Zac on the other side.

Alma shakes her head.

ALMA
I'm not sure they aren't working together still. It's pretty convenient that you can barely move.

MARTIN
She had to do that to fight infection.

ALMA
Zac said the same thing. Don't they both want to gain control over this creature and bend it to their own wills?

MARTIN
It's a creature now, is it?

ALMA
Her aim is the same. To trick and exploit the land. I don't see any good in that. However you achieve it.

Martin looks over and sees a figure.

He gets Alma's attention and points to the figure...

He creeps towards it. Trying to stay hidden until he is close enough to speak.

MARTIN
Hello?

Alma moves over to him

ALMA
What is it?

MARTIN
Someone in the woods. Can you see them?

Alma peers into the darkness of the trees.

They carefully move towards the figure. Alma going one way, Martin the other. They sneak up on the static figure.

As they get closer they realize it is one of Zac's wooden costumes. The face is made of a complicated weave of twigs.

MARTIN (CONT'D)
What does it mean?

ALMA
That Zac can attack us at any time.

EXT. WENDLE'S CAMP - MORNING - DAY 11.

Martin is tying a rope around the Hazmat suit. Doctor Wendle watches from her tent.

MARTIN
If you pass out, I can pull you back.

ALMA
Ok. I get through the mist. I go straight back to the camp. I can be there and back in a few days.

EXT. FOREST - DAY 11.

They three walk to the edge of the mist. Alma frowns as they arrive.

ALMA
It's moved.

MARTIN
How can you tell?

ALMA
I marked the edge of it. It's moved at least 5 meters.

DOCTOR WENDLE
It's made the mist belt deeper. To account for the effect of the mask.

Martin shakes his head. The forest can understand how the mask works? Really?

MARTIN
Ok, you ready?

Alma suits up.

ALMA
Ready.

MARTIN
Be careful. Please. I've already lost you once.

Alma smiles then walks into the woods.

MARTIN (CONT'D)
Keep talking on the coms.

ALMA ON COMS
Ok. Twenty paces in.

Martin and Doctor Wendle watch Alma disappear into the trees.

ALMA ON COMS (CONT'D)
I can't see anything. It's difficult going. The branches are thick… No sign of ill effects, though I'm feeling a bit anxious.

MARTIN
Keep going. You must be almost there.

ALMA ON COMS
It's getting harder now.

DOCTOR WENDLE
Tell her to come back.

ALMA ON COMS
I'm tired… I don't know why. Oh… What is that?… Stay away… What?…

DOCTOR WENDLE
Pull her back in!

MARTIN
Alma, are you okay?

ALMA ON COMS
Theres something in here with me… I can hear it…

MARTIN
Come back...

ALMA ON COMS
I can't find my way, I'm lost... Oh no... Something... Oh...

Alma starts screaming.

DOCTOR WENDLE
For god's sake pull her back in.

Martin starts to pull on the rope... Alma starts to appear in the mist. Martin and Doctor Wendle pull her clear. Wendle pulls the mask off. Alma is glassy eyed. She staggers to her feet and drinks some water.

MARTIN
What did you see?

ALMA
I saw a figure. But. I. I don't know. It was huge. It was everything.

DOCTOR WENDLE
She is delirious. I told you the filters wouldn't work

Wendle doesn't want to hear it. She moves away.

ALMA
It's not what they are saying.

MARTIN
In what way?

ALMA
I think she is thinking about it in the wrong way... there was a figure... but it's just pretending to be human... for us.

EXT. WENDLE'S CAMP - NIGHT - DAY 11.

Martin stands at the edge of the mist with Alma. She rubs her face.

Doctor Wendle walks over.

DOCTOR WENDLE
How far has it moved?

MARTIN
Another 10 meters. At this rate it will cover the camp by the morning.

They look over and see Zac standing at the perimeter. He is at the tree line, staring. They look back for a moment.

Martin stares at him.

MARTIN (CONT'D)
What do you want?

Zac stands and stares. He beckons to Doctor Wendle. She looks at Martin.

DOCTOR WENDLE
I need to talk to him.

Martin shakes his head.

DOCTOR WENDLE (CONT'D)
This is important. I've never seen him come this close to the camp.
He won't hurt me.

She walks over to the tree line. Martin watches nervously.
Alma joins him.

Doctor Wendle and Zac talk out of earshot. Zac looks over to Martin as he is speaking.

ALMA
What are they talking about?

Doctor Wendle walks back.

DOCTOR WENDLE
It wants to talk.

PART 5

THE FOREST

EXT. FOREST - NIGHT - DAY 11.

Doctor Wendle, Alma and Martin set out with equipment. Plugging in speakers. Checking batteries. Alma plugs in a cable next to Martin.

EXT. CAMP - NIGHT - DAY 11.

Alma and Martin sits with the doctor at her laptop as she turns on the communication array.

Wendle turns on the bass. It throbs through the woods. On her monitor she hears the forest throb back. We see the swirling heart of the forest represented in video form. The doctor gets out the book.

DOCTOR WENDLE
One of us has to go to the standing stone. That will be where all the sound and light activity will be focused. Then they need to take the sacrament.

ALMA
I thought that you were going to use your equipment to make contact with it?

DOCTOR WENDLE
Yes.

ALMA
But then why are you referring to this?

She points at the book.

DOCTOR WENDLE
Because it is the most direct route. It worked before.

ALMA
It broke Zac.

DOCTOR WENDE
Zac was not the right fit.

ALMA
I'm just struggling to understand why you are going to use ritual? We don't even know what tradition this comes from… This could be just made-up nonsense.

DOCTOR WENDLE
I've seen it work.

ALMA
And after this it will release us?

DOCTOR WENDLE
That is what Zac said.

MARTIN
I can't believe we are performing a ritual.

DOCTOR WENDLE
I understand this is uncomfortable for you, Martin, it's uncomfortable for me too. But if it wants to talk, we should listen.

ALMA
Ever thought for minute what it wants to say to you?

DOCTOR WENDLE
I would have thought that would be clear. How we can all live together, without de-

stroying each other. It's like any creature, it's worried about its environment, food, shelter.

ALMA
You are talking about it as if it's human. Isn't that what Zac thinks?

DOCTOR WENDLE
We are at the forefront of human discovery. Don't you think that we should endeavor to talk to this creature whatever the cost?

EXT. FOREST - NIGHT - DAY 11.

Alma and Martin walk towards the standing stone. Every sense is heightened. They can hear the grass under their feet. The branches move in the trees. Alma stops Martin.

ALMA
You don't have to do this.

Martin looks at her, smiles.

MARTIN
Let me do this. You saved my life. Let me return the favor if I can.

ALMA
It wasn't a favor and you don't need to pay it back.

Martin drinks back the Mycorrhiza spore drink that Doctor Wendle prepared.

DOCTOR WENDLE ON COMS
Martin, can you hear me?

MARTIN
Yes.

DOCTOR WENDLE ON COMS
Now we wait.

Black

Time passes.

DOCTOR WENDLE ON COMS (CONT'D)
What can you see out there?

MARTIN
I can't see anything. I mean, I can see shapes from the strobes.

DOCTOR WENDLE ON COMS
Stay focused on my voice.

In the forest the puffballs emit their spores.

Doctor Wendle pushes the sliders up on her mixing desk. The noise is overwhelming.

MARTIN
Arrrrgh… god.

Alma looks nervous.

DOCTOR WENDLE ON COMS
I'm sorry. Too loud.

She sets the level lower and tries again.

DOCTOR WENDLE ON COMS (CONT'D)
Is that better?

The doctor looks at her laptop. She slides a slider and the speakers crackle.

The woods are flooded by a deep bass sound.

The woods are silent for a moment. Then there is a slight wind and a crackle of branches.

Wendle looks at the results and smiles. She starts

pounding the forest with bass. She fires off the strobe lights again with bass tones.

EXT. FOREST - NIGHT - DAY 11.

The branches move and the forest seems to sigh. Strobes fire in different parts of the forest. The light bounces off the leaves. Highlighting the textures of the bark. Casting long shadows.
The deep booming of the bass echoes around the ancient wood.

EXT. WENDLE'S CAMP - NIGHT - DAY 11.

Doctor Wendle watches the readouts. The feedback plays back through the monitor speaker.

Small at first. But getting louder and deeper. Then there is short and the speakers and strobes go down.

Martin collapses holding his head.

MARTIN
Arrrrgh.

DOCTOR WENDLE ON COMS
Something has tripped the electrics.

ALMA
Any idea where?

DOCTOR WENDLE ON COMS
Lamp 15. Can you check it, Alma?

Alma moves off towards the blown light.

EXT. WENDLE'S CAMP - NIGHT - DAY 11.

Doctor Wendle restarts the amp. On her microphone.

DOCTOR WENDLE ON SPEAKERS
Can you hear me?

EXT. FOREST LAMP 15 - NIGHT - DAY 11.

Alma arrives at lamp 15. It's been smashed.

ALMA
It looks like someone has knocked it over.

She suddenly realizes what has happened. Zac.

ALMA (CONT'D)
Oh no.

But it is too late. Someone hits her hard from behind. She slumps to the ground.

EXT. FOREST - NIGHT - DAY 11.

Martin pulls himself up from the ground.

A figure steps out of the woods. Zac.

Martin struggles against Zac but he is too strong. He punches Martin in the guts.

The world is spinning and he collapses back down.

Black.

Martin starts to come too. He can see Zac holding a knife.

EXT. FOREST LAMP 15 - NIGHT - DAY 11.

Alma comes too. She touches the back of her head. Theres a lot of blood. She pulls herself up. The strobes and music pound through the woods.

EXT. WENDLE'S CAMP - NIGHT - DAY 11.

Alma runs to where she thinks that Doctor Wendle should be at the computer. But she is gone. The sounds are playing automated. She looks around and sees that a light is flickering in the third tent. The sound of deep bass.

Alma moves towards the tent.

She sees candles dancing about inside.

EXT. FOREST - NIGHT - DAY 11.

Zac has the knife to Martin's neck.

ZAC
She didn't tell you about the whole ritual did she?

Zac smiles. He whispers into Martin's ear.

ZAC (CONT'D)
Mycorrhiza always asks a price from its host. Your death will help her speak with it.

MARTIN
I don't understand…

ZAC
I wish it could be me, Martin. I would have given anything to have been the one…

It wouldn't take me… It called me but it wouldn't take me…

INT. TENT - NIGHT - DAY 11.

Alma pulls back the opening and sees inside for the first time.

Candles. Twigs. Bones. Photographs.

Doctor Wendle has the Hammer of the Witches open. Reading the ritual.

Doctor Wendle turns, wide-eyed.

ZAC (O.S)
NOW??

She see photographs that Zac has taken. Alma And Zac posed.

Alma staggers into the control desk. The mic turns on. Squarking feedback across the forest

DOCTOR WENDLE
I told you not to come back here.

She pulls out a knife

EXT. STANDING STONE - NIGHT - DAY 11.

Martin and Zac can hear the fight that is happening at the camp on the speakers. Zac throws Martin to the ground and heads back to the camp.
Martin's eyes roll to the back of his head.

EXT. FOREST - NIGHT - DAY 9.

Zac runs through the woods. He can hear the struggle. It's hard to say who is winning.

EXT. WENDLE'S CAMP - NIGHT - DAY 11.

Zac comes out of the woods.
The camp is empty… There are signs of a struggle. He looks around.

ZAC
Alma?

He sees Doctor Wendle on the ground. He goes over to her.

ZAC (CONT'D)
Where is she?

He turns too late. Alma hits him with a heavy torch.

Alma fights Zac, holding the torch as a club. The light swirls about. Dust us kicked up and it swirls in the beam. She shines it in his face.

Alma picks up a strobe light and turns it on. She dials it up high and uses it to drive Zac back.

Alma looks around for a weapon, pulls up a tent peg.

Zac claws at the light, but it's too much.

Alma drives the tent peg through Zac's eye.

He looks at her, shocked, for a moment. He staggers back and tries to pull it out. His eye bulges and he grips the peg. Alma watches in horror. Zac is in agony. He has another attempt at tentatively pulling it out. As he touches it, Alma smacks his hand with the torch and pushes it further in.

He collapses dead.

Alma looks around but Doctor Wendle is gone.

EXT. FOREST - NIGHT - DAY 11.

Doctor Wendle. The shadow of the stone is across her. She looks down and sees Martin.

The strobes fire. The bass booms. She holds Martin's head.

DOCTOR WENDLE
What can you see?

Martin's vision is blurred. She sits down next to him and pulls out her knife. She puts it to Martin's throat.

DOCTOR WENDLE (CONT'D)
I wasn't surprised when I saw you here, Martin. It made sense that the forest would call you.
You were so open, so trusting, it can see that in you, perfect for a vessel.

This is the most important moment in your life.

She starts to cut into Martin's neck. Martin grabs her hand but he doesn't have much strength.

MARTIN
Please.

DOCTOR WENDLE
You have to go willingly… this is your moment, Martin.

Alma gets to the standing stone, the mist is moving in.

Alma pulls Doctor Wendle off of Martin and tries to pull him out.

ALMA
Come on. Martin, don't go.

Doctor Wendle stands up and crushes two puffballs into her face and walks, hands open, into the mist

DOCTOR WENDLE
Take me…

The mist rolls in over her…

Alma can't pull Martin out fast enough. The mist engulfs her as well.

ALMA
Hold on, Martin. Don't go.

Martin feels something pulling at his sanity. The massiveness of the creature that lives in the forest.

He is being taken apart by its ancient intelligence.

Alma sees something beyond our realm, for a moment is one with trees. Sees the roots and the capillaries of the land. Spreading out like a circuit board. The figure approaches her as it did Zac, but she does not resist it. She welcomes it.

Is it Parnag Fegg? Released from his millennia trapped in the forest. Or is it something more fundamental. A connection between humans and the land?

The figure moves towards her. In the light. It spreads its arms to welcome her.

This intense moment lasts for minute or so of screentime. A kaleidoscope of memory and sense. Of Alma and Martin being broken down and re-assembled.

The sound and light are used here to represent the forest language. Instead of us looking from the outside in, we are fully inside the experience now.

And

It

Is

Beautiful

And

Terrifying.

A crescendo. Then calm. Water. Breeze.

EXT. WENDLE'S CAMP - GLOAMING - DAY 12.

The light rises. The sun is over the horizon. Orange light. The strobes become less bright now.

The sun pokes through orange. Blues and purples wrap around the edges of the land.

Quiet now. Echoes decay from the speakers. Just breathing. It is quiet now. The forest is resting. Alma walks into the woods. Crunch of twigs underfoot. Leaves blow. Birds. The figure has gone now. The wood is back to normal.

EXT. FOREST - GLOAMING - DAY 12.

Doctor Wendle is standing, looking out into space. Her expression blank. She is lost inside her mind.

Martin is on the ground, still unconscious.
Alma leans down to him and gets him to drink. He opens his eyes and looks up at her.

ALMA
How can I help you, traveller?

She pulls him to his feet.

ALMA (CONT'D)
Let me guide you out of the woods.

Martin looks into her eyes. She is Alma and something else. Something ancient.

REPEATER BOOKS

is dedicated to the creation of a new reality. The landscape of twenty-first-century arts and letters is faded and inert, riven by fashionable cynicism, egotistical self-reference and a nostalgia for the recent past. Repeater intends to add its voice to those movements that wish to enter history and assert control over its currents, gathering together scattered and isolated voices with those who have already called for an escape from Capitalist Realism. Our desire is to publish in every sphere and genre, combining vigorous dissent and a pragmatic willingness to succeed where messianic abstraction and quiescent co-option have stalled: abstention is not an option: we are alive and we don't agree.